CONSTITUTIONAL LAW AND LIABILITY FOR AGENTS, DEPUTIES, AND POLICE OFFICERS

By

Dan S. Murrell, J.D., LL.M.
Cecil C. Humphreys School of Law
Memphis State University
Memphis, Tennessee 38152

and

William O. Dwyer, Ph.D.
Center for Applied Psychological Research
Department of Psychology
Memphis State University
Memphis, Tennessee 38152

Carolina Academic Press
Durham, North Carolina

ACKNOWLEDGMENTS

The authors are very grateful for the help of all those law enforcement officers, attorneys, graduate students, and others who assisted us with advice, suggestions, and counsel during the development of this work.

We wish to especially thank Lisa Coleman and Christina Douglas for their assistance in research, and Susan Vazquez for her help in editing the manuscript.

ISBN 0-89089-521-X
LCCN 92-73633
Copyright 1992 Dan S. Murrell and William O. Dwyer

Printed in the United States of America

TO ORDER COPIES, CONTACT:
Carolina Academic Press
700 Kent Street
Durham, North Carolina 27701
(919)489-7486   FAX (919)493-5668

TO THE READER------

This book is intended to help you, the reader, but we also need your help to insure that it meets your needs. If you have any suggestions, questions, problems, or situations that need to be addressed, please let us know so that we may consider those problems for future editions. We will try to respond individually to your correspondence.

We would like to know about your particular jurisdiction's laws, statutes, and regulations and will address those whenever possible in the future.

Any correspondence should be sent to either of the authors:

Professor Dan S. Murrell
Cecil C. Humphreys School of Law
Memphis State University
Memphis, Tennessee 38152
(901) 678-3219

or

Professor William O. Dwyer
Center for Applied Psychological Research
Department of Psychology
Memphis State University
Memphis, Tennessee 38152
(901) 678-2149

NOTE: Blank pages have been left at appropriate intervals for your notes and questions.

TABLE OF CONTENTS

TABLE OF CASES

CHAPTER 1

INTRODUCTION

During the past 30 years, American society has increasingly demanded that the police delineate and restrict their role as agents of authority. The Supreme Court has reflected these demands and, through the vehicle of selective incorporation, has used case law to apply most of the guarantees in the Bill of Rights to state actions as well as federal. While some are of the opinion that these judicial decisions have "tied the hands of the police," others feel that they have encouraged the police to become more "professional." Whatever the perspective, effective law enforcement in America requires an adherence to constitutional mandates and guidelines. If law enforcement officers violate these guidelines in their dealings with the public, they face the potential consequences of suppressed evidence as well as personal criminal and civil liability. Furthermore, this liability may extend to their supervisors and the agencies for which they work.

The purpose of this book is to provide a quick and handy reference for law enforcement officers on how the Constitution, as interpreted through various court decisions, influences their contacts with the public. Our intention is to present a sound framework against which the practice of law enforcement may be measured. The book is not meant to be a complete list of "Do's and Don'ts" because various state laws and local regulations, as well as agency guidelines and procedures, may also have a bearing on the breadth of enforcement authority given police officers. Therefore, where more restrictive guidelines are in place, the reader is cautioned to make a note of them.

NOTES

CHAPTER 2

LIABILITY AND CIVIL RIGHTS

A. BACKGROUND

Of all the Supreme Court cases delimiting the scope of acceptable law enforcement behaviors, those which increased police exposure to criminal and civil liability for violation of civil rights have probably had the most impact on police procedures. If in its zeal to protect the public and its property, law enforcement unnecessarily impinges on individuals' civil rights or their expectations of privacy, the public is increasingly likely to seek legal redress for what it perceives as a violation of its prerogatives.

These factors add up to a requirement for the professional and temperate use of police powers by law enforcement personnel. Of the various means created for guaranteeing the protection of the public's constitutional rights, criminal and civil liability are of the greatest concern to officers and administrators.

Although the Supreme Court has held that law enforcement officers enjoy a certain "qualified good-faith immunity" from liability for their actions, they may still be held criminally and civilly liable if they act outside the scope of their employment, violate their agency's guidelines, or violate a person's civil rights.

B. CRIMINAL LIABILITY

Federal as well as state statutes make it a criminal offense for anyone acting in the capacity of a public law enforcement officer to willfully violate an individual's civil rights that are guaranteed by the United States Constitution or federal law. For example, Title 18 of the United States Code, Section 242, makes it illegal for an officer acting under color of law to willfully subject any inhabitant of a state, territory or district to the "deprivation of any rights, privileges or immunities secured or protected by the Constitution or laws of the United States..." Police officers who willfully and with intent violate someone's civil rights may be convicted of a crime and imprisoned. For this to occur, they would have to be proven guilty beyond a reasonable doubt.

C. CIVIL LIABILITY

Federal as well as state governments have established provisions for people who have been deprived of their civil rights by officers acting under color of law to sue those officers in civil court for compensation for any loss (including loss of a right) or harm which may have resulted from the deprivation. Title 42, Section 1983 of the United States Code, for example, states that anyone acting under color of law who "subjects, or causes to be subjected, any citizen of the United States or other person within the jurisdiction thereof to the deprivation of any rights, privileges or immunities secured by the Constitution and laws, shall be liable to the party injured in an action at law, lawsuit in equity, or other proper proceeding for redress." To be successful in such a suit, a plaintiff would not have to prove willfulness on the part of the officer, and the level of proof required in civil matters is merely "a preponderance of the evidence," not "beyond a reasonable doubt."

The figure below bears ample testimony that Americans are discovering the potential effectiveness of the §1983 remedy to alleged abuse by government officials.

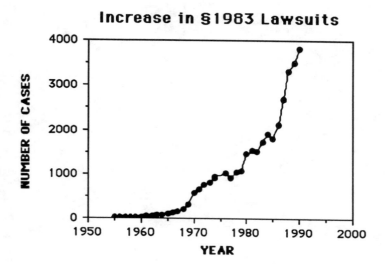

Number of §1983 cases in the federal
courts from 1955 through 1990

NOTES

CHAPTER 3

REVIEW OF POLICE POWERS

A. THE CONSTITUTION AND POLICE AUTHORITY

In the past thirty years, the Supreme Court has energetically articulated (and restricted) the latitude within which law enforcement officers may exercise their police authority. The Court's decisions have had a significant impact on police behavior. Most of these decisions have had their foundations in the first eight of the ten amendments, known as the Bill of Rights. Of the 23 rights guaranteed in these eight Amendments, 12 have a direct bearing on criminal procedure, and of these, the Fourth, Fifth, and Sixth Amendments are the most relevant for law enforcement.

The **Fourth Amendment** (1) protects people against unreasonable searches and seizures, and (2) restricts the conditions under which warrants may be issued. The **Fifth Amendment** (1) requires a grand jury in criminal cases, (2) protects against double jeopardy, and (3) prohibits a person from being forced to testify against himself or herself. The **Sixth Amendment** addresses the rights of individuals in criminal prosecutions: (1) the right to a speedy and public trial, (2) the right to an impartial jury, (3) the right to be informed of the charges against the defendant, (4) the right to subpoena witnesses, (5) the right to confront the accuser, and (6) the right to counsel.

Although the **First Amendment** does not bear directly on criminal procedure as such, it does guarantee five specific rights, two of which are quite relevant to law enforcement activities: (1) freedom of speech, and (2) freedom of peaceable assembly. This amendment may also protect an individual's right to freely exercise his or her religion. The Court has traditionally relied, in part, on the First Amendment to support the right to privacy.

7

What follows in this book is an elaboration of how the courts' interpretations of some of these rights have established the limits on what you as a law enforcement officer are able to do in your role as an agent of authority.

B. OFFICER AUTHORITY

What are police powers?

Police powers are inherent in the state governmental function and are granted to the federal government by the United States Constitution; they provide the authority and responsibility for designated governmental entities to provide for peace and order, to enforce the law, to detain and arrest others, and to seize property as evidence pursuant to knowledge of the commission of some crime.

What is the difference between the arrest power of citizens and that of public law enforcement officers?

Citizens possess the right to arrest perpetrators of crimes, but if after such an arrest, it is determined that the arrestee did not commit the crime, or the state does not prosecute, the arresting citizen may be liable for false arrest. On the other hand, a law enforcement officer employed by a public entity has certain immunities from such liability. Unlike the citizen who must have absolute knowledge (unless given special statutory authority) that the person to be arrested actually committed the crime, all that is required of a law enforcement officer (i.e., a person who is operating under color of law) is that he or she had probable cause to believe that a crime was committed and the person arrested committed it. Minor variations may exist among different jurisdictions.

tions you have your police powers whether in or out of uniform.

What is my authority in special enclaves that may be within my jurisdiction (i.e., special state or federal holdings)?

The state or federal government may own property within your jurisdiction over which it maintains exclusive control, leaving you with no police authority on this property. Examples include some federal or state parks, military installations, post offices, state universities, or similar institutions. These entities may extend your authority to an enclave by agreement or invitation.

D. LAWS AND REGULATIONS

Police officers may be given the responsibility of enforcing both laws and regulations, sometimes of more than one jurisdiction.

What are criminal laws?

Criminal Laws designate certain acts or failures to act as being illegal and provide specific punishments for them. To be enacted, laws must be passed by either state or federal legislatures (depending upon jurisdiction) or have uncontested common law existence at the state level.

What are regulations?

Regulations may also articulate limits on behavior and may carry penalties of fines and imprisonment. Unlike laws, however, regulations are not specifically enacted by a legislature; rather they are promulgated by an agency (e.g., the Department of Justice, state bureau of investigation, or sherrif's department). Of course, the agency depends on legislation for its right to promulgate such regulations. Regulations can have the force and effectiveness of law; that is, their violation can lead to legal action, arrest, fines, and imprisonment. Governmental entities often operate under special legislative enactments and will decree special rules and regulations that will usually give additional authority to its police personnel.

E. DEADLY FORCE

RULE OF LAW: Deadly force may not be used to effect an arrest. It may be used only to protect yourself or others from imminent lethal force or severe injury.

For all police, the question of when deadly force may be employed is fairly simple to answer; it may be applied only in defense of the officer's life or someone else's. Until 1985 some states allowed officers to shoot to apprehend fleeing felons. Since 1985, however, the Supreme Court has ruled that shooting a fleeing felon merely to prevent escape is a violation of civil rights.

Under what conditions may I use deadly force?

Specifically, the Supreme Court restricted the use of deadly force to situations of (1) defense of the officer's life, (2) defense of others' lives, or (3) when the officer has probable cause to believe that the suspect has committed a violent crime involving the infliction or threat of death or serious harm, or probable cause to believe that the suspect is armed and poses an imminent substantial risk to others. To be protected by qualified good faith immunity, you must follow the established deadly force policy of your agency. If you are using deadly force (in accordance with policy) to stop a person under condition (3) above, you must exhaust all other reasonable means of apprehension and, whenever possible, identify yourself and warn suspects that if they do not stop you will use deadly force.

Should I "shoot to kill"?

You should not use deadly force except in the situations noted above. If the situation mandates the use of deadly force, you should shoot to stop the individual from inflicting deadly force or serious bodily harm on another.

What are the implications of these restrictions on the use of deadly force for Special Weapons and Tactics (SWAT) teams?

SWAT teams are permitted **no** greater latitude in the use of deadly force than any other law enforcement officer. SWAT teams, however, are routinely employed under extreme circumstances that normally involve threats to life and the display of weapons. Accordingly, these incidents may necessitate increased force. However, deadly force may **not** be employed by SWAT teams merely to conclude an incident or effect an arrest.

SWAT teams should always be employed under a strict command structure, be thoroughly disciplined and trained, and function only pursuant to written standard operating procedures.

May deadly force be used by a SWAT team to effect the release of a hostage?

As a rule, negotiations and other non-violent means should be attempted prior to using force to conclude a hostage incident, and deadly force should not be employed merely for the purpose of accomplishing the release of a hostage. Deadly force may be appropriate in those circumstances where the hostage or the officers attempting to gain the release of the hostage are in imminent danger of harm.

NOTES

May I check the VIN during a stop at a roadblock?

Yes, you may check the VIN (vehicle identification number) during any lawful stop whether at a roadblock or not. You may reach into the vehicle and move objects covering the VIN plate, and any evidence, fruits or instrumentalities of a crime discovered in the course of such action may be properly seized. The stop, under appropriate circumstances, such as looking for a particular stolen vehicle, may even be to check the VIN number.

May I establish a roadblock/checkpoint to stop every vehicle to check for an intoxicated driver?

Yes. Usually referred to as "OUI (DWI) checkpoints," they may be legally established to allow you to briefly stop every vehicle and talk to the driver to make sure he or she is sober enough to drive.

What are the conditions and restrictions of such a checkpoint?

To make sure that your checkpoint is being conducted in a manner consistent with guidelines enumerated by the Supreme Court, you should do the following:

a.   Make a public announcement (e.g., in local newspapers) that you will be conducting such stops over the next few weeks/months.
b.   Establish a written policy detailing the conduct of such checkpoints.
c.   Obtain written directives from management for each checkpoint occurrence, detailing exactly where, when, and for what duration the checkpoint will be conducted.
d.   Establish checkpoint locations that will maximize safety for the officers and motorists. Clearly identify them with signs, traffic cones, and adequate lighting.
e.   Stops should be brief and courteous, requiring only a short conversation during which the officer can look for signs of intoxication, such as presence of alcohol in

vehicle, odor of an intoxicating beverage, quality of speech, general demeanor, etc.

f. If, based upon these observations, your suspicion is aroused that the driver may be intoxicated, the stop should then proceed as any other OUI (DWI) traffic stop.

g. Be sure to have adequate manpower present to handle more than one vehicle at a time, or any arrests, vehicle impoundments, etc. that may be required.

h. Do not let your checkpoint develop into a traffic jam. Drivers should not have to wait very long for you to contact them. If such a condition begins developing, it is wise to wave all of them through without contacting them.

3. **Waterblocks**

If my jurisdiction has a problem with people boating while under the influence of alcohol, may I conduct "waterblocks" during which I check boat operators for sobriety?

Yes. You may conduct waterblocks for "boating under the influence," using the same basic criteria you would for roadblock OUI checkpoints. In addition to the other requirements, it would be wise to post a notice at area boat ramps informing boaters that you periodically conduct such stops. Remember that if you obtain reasonable suspicion that a boat operator may be intoxicated, the typical field sobriety tests requiring balance may be less useful on the water. Other types of tests should be considered.

B. FRISKING A SUSPECT

RULE OF LAW: During a stop, you may conduct a frisk to protect yourself or others if you have a reasonable suspicion that the individual stopped may be armed and dangerous.

1. Individual

A frisk of an individual is a patdown of the outer clothing for the sole purpose of looking for **weapons**. A frisk may also extend to the inside of an over garment, such as an overcoat. You may use the minimum reasonable force, excluding deadly force, necessary to compel submission to the frisk. For example, this may include the use of handcuffs if they are necessary to restrain the suspect during a frisk.

What is "reasonable force?"

Reasonable force is that amount which is minimally necessary and which would be used by a reasonable and prudent officer to gain compliance from a suspect. Any amount of force above this level would be considered **punishment** and would, therefore, be excessive.

When may I frisk an individual whom I have stopped?

You may frisk suspects whom you have stopped only if you have a **reasonable** (that is, articulable) suspicion that they may be armed and that they may harm you or others. You do not need probable cause, but neither is a "hunch" or a "feeling" sufficient. Reasonable suspicion for a frisk is established essentially by a combination of the suspect's demeanor and the bulkiness of the clothing being worn.

a. Articles taken during a frisk

What may I remove from a person whom I am frisking?

You may remove only those items that you reasonably suspect could be weapons. Examples would be: guns, knives, brass knuckles, hair picks, screwdrivers and other tools, bottles, chains, etc. If, however, an object you believe to be a weapon is removed, but is not a weapon, yet it is evidence or fruits of a crime, it may be seized. Any item removed pursuant to a valid frisk, or observed in plain view during the frisk, that is evidence of a crime, may be used to support a subsequent arrest or warrant. Remember, you are responsible for any objects taken, and the individual should be told where he or she may recover them later, if they are not illegal to possess.

During an administrative frisk, anything that is the object of the frisk may be taken (e.g., alcoholic beverages).

If, during a frisk, I feel something soft in a pocket, may I remove it?

No. A frisk is a patdown for weapons, only. As an example, while frisking a suspect, you feel something soft, remove it from the person's pocket, and it turns out to be cocaine. If you then arrested the suspect on a narcotics charge, the evidence seized may be suppressed at trial. Under some circumstances, however, the evidence may be used to support a grand jury indictment or search warrant. In any event, you may confiscate the cocaine because the individual may not lawfully possess it.

b. Frisking others

If I stop and frisk a person, may I frisk others who are with him or her?

You may frisk them if you believe that they are dangerous to you or others and that they may interfere with your initial stop and its purpose. The mere presence of others at the stop or frisk, however, does not necessarily justify a frisk of them.

c. Frisking the opposite sex

Is it permissible to frisk a suspect of the opposite sex?

From a constitutional perspective, there are no prohibitions against frisking persons of the opposite sex other than those

26

rules which govern the frisking of any suspect. It is important, however, to keep in mind that you should never do anything that a court may consider sufficiently shocking or offensive to social norms, because it could result in your losing the case. Of course, you should abide by any additional guidelines that your agency may have on this issue. Do remember the purpose of frisking and act accordingly.

2. Area around suspect

You may extend the frisk to the immediate area around the stopped individual if you feel that he or she is dangerous and may be able to reach a weapon. This extension is solely for the purpose of looking for a weapon. You might, for example, pat down or reach and grab a weapon on the floor of an automobile, or on a blanket if it is in close proximity. The allowable extent of your search is essentially determined by the "jump and reach" rule (see Chapter 7).

3. Examining possessions

If the suspect is in possession of a book satchel, brief case, attaché case, shopping bag, or backpack, may I look in these items for weapons during a frisk?

Generally the answer would be "No." You could frisk the pack for **weapons**, but you may not search for other items without additional cause. The frisk may be extended to a patdown of a bedroll, backpack, etc. The frisk may be used to remove legal weapons (e.g., a knife), if you believe that such a course of action is reasonably necessary for your own protection during the stop. If you remove a legal weapon you must, of course, tell the person where it may be recovered.

NOTES

CHAPTER 5

ARRESTING A SUSPECT

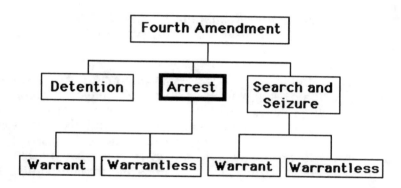

A. BACKGROUND

1. What is an arrest?

You have arrested a person when you have deprived him or her of freedom to come and go by taking him or her into custody. Whether an arrest has been made is determined from the circumstances. The courts routinely say that an arrest may have been made if several officers are standing around a person, the officer's weapon is drawn, the person is taken to headquarters, etc. Obviously, a person is under arrest if told so; however, words are not necessary, as actions may indicate the occurrence of an arrest.

A person is not under arrest if he or she volunteers to come to headquarters or to a police station to make a statement and then is free to leave.

May I arrest or restrain an individual who is displaying abnormal or dangerous behavior?

You may take a person into custody for his or her own protection if the person is exhibiting dangerous or abnormal behavior. The individual should be transported immediately to a medical facility and released to appropriate medical person-

29

nel. It would be wise to complete a report concerning such an incident. A scenario of this type will not generally be considered an arrest.

Once I have arrested someone, may I release that person myself without the intervention of some judicial authority?

There is no process of unarrest. As a rule an arrested individual should be taken before a magistrate or judge within 48 hours, and any release is within the prerogative of the court. You may release an individual on your own initiative; however, you must be careful of the process because false arrest charges could be raised. Of course, if you have merely stopped a person for investigation, releasing that individual is not a problem.

What is the difference between an arrest and a temporary investigative detention?

A temporary detention for investigation is exactly that — temporary or of short duration. The person is either quickly released or is arrested. During a detention a "Terry" type frisk may be used to look for weapons if you have reason to believe that the suspect may be armed and dangerous.

An arrest involves depriving a person of freedom to come and go, that is, seizing the person. The arrest must be justified if you expect it to continue.

If I issue a citation, is that essentially the same thing as an arrest?

No, not unless you intend it to be and make the arrest pursuant to the probable cause giving rise to the citation, or other facts appear giving rise to probable cause for an arrest. To make an arrest, physical custody must be involved. You may not search incident to a citation.

If I overtly initiate an arrest (such as handcuffing), and during the course of the confrontation I decide that merely writing a citation would suffice, may I write the citation and release the subject?

Yes. However, if you release such an individual, there is an element of liability present for false arrest. This demonstrates the need for being prudent in making an arrest decision.

2. Why arrest?

What are the reasons for arresting a suspect?

In general, you would arrest a person whom you have probable cause to believe has committed a felony, or one who has committed a misdemeanor in your presence, and if you can satisfy any of the three following reasons: (1) to guarantee the person's presence in court, (2) to protect the person or someone else from physical harm, or (3) to prevent the loss or destruction of evidence of the crime. You should **not** arrest a violator "just to teach a lesson."

3. Requirements for an arrest

What are the requirements for a lawful arrest?

You must have the authority, you must be in the appropriate jurisdiction, and you must have a warrant or probable cause to believe that a crime was committed and the person you are about to arrest was the perpetrator.

Do I need a warrant to make an arrest?

In spite of the "warrant requirement" of the Fourth Amendment, you generally do not need a warrant to make a physical arrest for a felony or for a misdemeanor committed in your presence. However, it is a very good idea to obtain a warrant if you have time.

What is the difference between a felony and a misdemeanor?

A **felony** is any offense for which the penalty may exceed more than one year in jail. A **misdemeanor** is any offense for which the penalty is less than one year in jail. A **petit offense** is a type of misdemeanor for which the penalty is further limited.

4. Personal jurisdiction

Personal jurisdiction involves an officer's having physical control (custody) over a subject for the purpose of the judicial process.

Personal jurisdiction of an individual within your jurisdiction may be obtained:

a. pursuant to an arrest
b. pursuant to a warrant
c. by consent or submission
d. by subpoena

Personal jurisdiction outside of your jurisdiction may be obtained:

a. by consent or submission
b. through a federal warrant for unlawful flight to avoid prosecution
c. by extradition

If I wish to obtain custody of a person who is outside of my jurisdictional boundary (e.g., over the state line), what should I do?

Absent emergency circumstances, the matter should be referred to appropriate local or national authorities.

Suppose that I am outside of my agency's juris-diction and observe a suspect whom I know is wanted for a felony in my jurisdiction. May I properly arrest that person and return him or her to my jurisdiction?

You may take the suspected felon into custody for the local authorities; then appropriate authorities may take action for extradition. When you take the suspect into custody, you should turn him or her over to local authorities as soon as possible.

How long may I hold an arrestee before I must take him or her before a judge or magistrate?

As a general rule an in-custody suspect must be taken before a magistrate as soon as possible, and in no event later than within 48 hours. Some examples of delays even within the 48 hours which are unreasonable are delays for the purpose of gathering additional evidence to justify the arrest, a delay motivated by ill will against the arrested individual, or delay for the delay's sake. The government upon demonstration of a *bona fide* emergency may obtain a brief extension, but delays for administrative purposes, hearing consolidations, or intervening weekends do not qualify as extraordinary circumstances. The individual does not bear the burden of proving unreasonable delay; rather the government bears the responsibility of proving a *bona fide* emergency or extraordinary circumstance was present. In general, unnecessary delays may create a risk of false arrest, kidnapping, and the suppression of evidence.

B. WARRANT ARRESTS

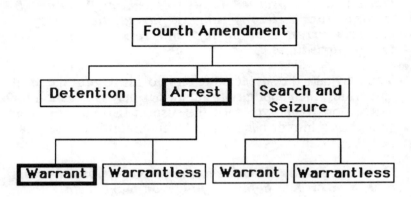

RULE OF LAW: A police officer may arrest any person believed to be named in a valid arrest warrant. This arrest may be pursuant to the knowledge of a warrant even though the warrant is not in hand.

What is an arrest warrant?

An arrest warrant is an order from the issuing court directing an officer or class of officers (e.g., any FBI agent) to carry out a particular action, such as take an individual into custody.

What do I need to obtain a warrant for an arrest?

In order to obtain an arrest warrant from a judicial officer (e.g., a judge or magistrate), you will have to demonstrate that you have probable cause for the suspect's arrest for a particular crime. The facts or apparent facts you use to develop your probable cause will have to be presented to the judicial officer in sworn testimony, usually accompanied by a written complaint or affidavit.

If a judge issues an arrest warrant based on the information I provided, am I immune from any liability for an unconstitutional arrest?

Not necessarily. The Court has held that you are granted qualified good-faith immunity only if a reasonable officer would have believed that the facts you presented were adequate to establish probable cause. Thus, a judge's signature on a warrant does not necessarily protect you from liability.

From whom may I obtain an arrest warrant?

Generally arrest warrants may be obtained by appearing before any judge, magistrate, or justice of the peace, regardless of jurisdiction. However, it is advisable to seek an arrest warrant from the judge or magistrate associated with your particular jurisdiction. Federal warrants normally require the judge or magistrate to be of a court of record (i.e., as opposed to a justice of the peace).

When must I have a warrant to make a physical arrest?

Unless it is a true emergency, you must have a warrant to make an arrest under the following conditions:

a. when you are arresting persons in their own home or in the dwelling of another where they have a right to be,

b. when you are making an arrest for a misdemeanor not committed in your presence.

What are the restrictions regarding the execution of warrants from other jurisdictions, or in other jurisdictions?

If you are inside your jurisdiction you may:

a. execute an arrest warrant issued for your jurisdiction for an offense committed in your jurisdiction,

b. hold a person for the proper authorities if you believe your jurisdiction or another jurisdiction issued an arrest warrant for a crime committed elsewhere. You should determine if the warrant is valid on its face (current, etc.).

If you are outside your jurisdiction but within your state you may, depending upon your authority:

a. execute an arrest warrant issued by your jurisdiction for an offense committed in your jurisdiction,

b. assist other officers in the execution of their warrants.

If you are outside your jurisdictional limits and outside your state you may:

a. not execute any arrest warrants unless you are a federal officer,

b. assist other officers in the execution of their warrants.

C. WARRANTLESS ARRESTS

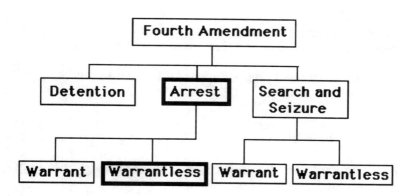

RULE OF LAW: A police officer may arrest, without a warrant, any person committing a misdemeanor in his or her presence or any person whom the officer has probable cause to believe has committed a felony.

Do I have to observe individuals actually committing an offense before I may arrest them for it?

In general, the answer is "No" for felonies and "Yes" for misdemeanors.

If I don't actually observe the felony, what can I use to establish probable cause to arrest the offender?

Any facts or apparent facts which lead you to reasonably believe that the offender probably committed the offense can help develop probable cause. Examples would be: testimonies of others, lying during questioning, furtive activities, difficulty in making a vehicle stop, the presence of burglar tools, a physical description, or the smell of an intoxicating beverage about an individual. When any one fact (or group of facts) makes you believe that (1) a specific crime was probably committed and (2) a given person probably was involved in committing it, then you have probable cause for an arrest.

May a "feeling" or a "hunch" I have about a person help develop probable cause for an arrest?

No. You must have facts or apparent facts with which to develop probable cause.

May I use a person's refusal to answer my questions to help develop probable cause for an arrest?

No. The exercise of a civil right should not be used to help develop the basis for an arrest.

Can an arrest be justified by what I discover after the arrest has been made?

No. You must obtain all the information necessary to establish probable cause for an arrest before it is made. For example, if you arrest a suspect without sufficient probable cause and subsequently discover that he has been selling cocaine on a street corner, that discovery will not validate the arrest.

Under what conditions may I make an arrest for a misdemeanor?

a. if the arrest is pursuant to a warrant,

b. if the misdemeanor was committed in your presence,

c. in some jurisdictions, if you have a witness' signed statement or affidavit,

d. under certain conditions in which it is obvious that a suspect committed the misdemeanor, such as finding a drunk behind the steering wheel of a wrecked vehicle. While you did not witness the accident, conditions are sufficiently strong to support an arrest. State statutes

What is the permissible extent of the search of a recreational vehicle incident to an arrest if the RV is parked?

The more stationary the vehicle, the more it will be treated as a premises and require a search warrant or exigent circumstances. The arrest of an individual in or nearby an RV will allow a search of the individual and the immediate area around the individual, as with any conventional arrest. For example, where a motor home is parked in a trailer court, and the driver is seated in a chair outside of the vehicle, the search would be of the driver and the immediate area around him. If, instead, he were seated inside his RV, the immediate area around him in the vehicle could be searched.

Are unusual vehicles subject to the same rules of search incident to arrest?

You may, incident to arrest, search all varieties of vehicles, including cycles, snowmobiles, all-terrain vehicles, etc.

3. **Boats:** You may search incident to an arrest a boat in the same manner that you would search a vehicle. The high mobility and visibility allow this search as is the case in conventional vehicle searches. Accordingly, the larger the vessel the more the search should be confined to the area around the arrestee.

You may search a larger vessel if you have probable cause to believe that it contains evidence that will be destroyed or lost if not seized immediately. The better approach would be to stop and detain the boat and obtain a search warrant as soon as possible.

May I search a fishing boat or speed boat pursuant to a stop for operation of the boat in an unsafe manner?

No, not without more. You must effect an arrest of the boat's operator or have probable cause to independently support the search. You may observe all items in plain view and use that observation to support a subsequent arrest or warrant. If you arrest the operator or other occupant, you may search the boat in the same manner as a vehicle. For example, you may search the tool compartment, ice chest, live well, or similar areas as long as they are not locked. You may not search a motor compartment or similarly removed area unless you have reason to believe that the area contains evidence, fruits, or instrumentalities of the crime.

Incident to the arrest of its operator, may I search a compartmentalized or cabin cruiser?

You may search the area immediately around the operator in the same manner as you would a recreation vehicle. The larger the vessel, the more restricted the area of the search. However, all items observed in plain view may be used to support an arrest or warrant. Likewise, those items may provide probable cause to extend the scope of the search. Obviously, a search warrant should be utilized if possible, and the vessel may be detained for a brief period of time to conduct a necessary investigation or to obtain a search warrant.

When arresting a person in a docked cabin cruiser or houseboat, may I search the vessel?

No. You may search the individual and the area immediately around him or her as in the search of a premises. The vessel should be treated as a premises with mobility and handled accordingly. The more likely that the boat will be moved, the more you may be able to justify a warrantless search. However, a warrant should be obtained whenever possible. You may detain the vessel for a brief period of time to obtain a warrant. Thus, a docked boat should be treated similarly to an RV in a campground.

4. **Aircraft**: The high mobility of aircraft allow them to be treated in the same manner as conventional vehicles. Accordingly, the arrest of the pilot or other occupant will permit a search of the person and the area immediately around him or her. In a small plane this would permit a

48

What is a search warrant?

A warrant is an order from the issuing court directing an officer or class of officers (e.g., any police officer) to carry out a particular action, such as conduct a search for illegal drugs or related paraphernalia.

From whom may I obtain a search warrant?

Like arrest warrants, search warrants may be obtained by appearing before any judge, magistrate, or justice of the peace, regardless of jurisdiction. However, it is advisable to seek an arrest warrant from the judge or magistrate associated with your particular jurisdiction. Federal warrants normally require the judge or magistrate to be of a court of record (i.e., as opposed to a justice of the peace).

What kinds of information may I use to establish probable cause for a search warrant?

You may use personal knowledge or observation, or information obtained from a reliable source that you believe to be accurate. The accuracy may be determined by your observation of events following the report of the informant. For example, a pedestrian approaches you and tells you that a particular individual appears to be selling drugs from a late model van. You observe that person handing a small package to another person. You may seek a search warrant for the vehicle, based on your informant's report and your observation.

May I obtain a search warrant by providing a judge with the necessary information over the telephone?

Although some jurisdictions may apply other restrictions, case and statutory law today generally allows telephonic warrants for circumstances in which it is impossible or impractical for you to physically appear before a judge or magistrate first. Of course, such warrant applications must eventually be supported by the same evidence or affidavit as any other warrant. The telephonic warrant should be used for urgent situations, not merely inconvenient ones.

What are the restrictions on a search with a warrant?

There are seven basic restrictions:

a. A member of the class of officers, (although he or she may be assisted by other officers) to whom the warrant is directed must be present at the search and should generally be the first to initiate execution (entry, etc.). As an example, a warrant directed to a police officer to search a building for drugs or evidence thereof should be carried out by at least one police officer, but he or she may be assisted by others, for example sheriff deputies, drug agents, etc.

b. The search warrant must be executed within a reasonable time period after its issuance. As a general rule, a week should be an adequate time to complete the execution of the warrant. Local rules will dictate the time of return of the warrant. If your warrant is not executed in a timely manner, a new warrant may be necessary. It is not uncommon for new evidence to be required to obtain a new warrant to replace a warrant not executed in a timely manner.

c. The search must take place in the particular location directed by the warrant. For example, a warrant to search for stolen audio-visual equipment in a house may be extended to those buildings at the address or location specified in the warrant that are in close proximity to the house. A warrant to search the garage for a stolen tractor, however, would not extend to other buildings, including the house.

d. The search must be for the particular item(s) specified in the warrant, and you may search only in places where the item(s) could reasonably be located. If you have a warrant for narcotics, you could look in all places where

and that the need was sufficient to proceed without a warrant.

b. **Boats**: Because of their mobility and visibility, boats are to be treated similarly to conventional vehicles in that the expectation of privacy is reduced. Vessels of the cabin variety should be treated as RVs or premises, as appropriate.

Boats may be boarded for safety inspections more readily than vehicles, due to the necessity of checking safety equipment such as fire extinguishers and life preservers. Any evidence observed in plain view may be seized and used to support an arrest or warrant. Obviously boats may be stopped for unsafe or reckless operation, for lack of running lights, etc.

Boats may also be stopped to inspect an operator's fishing or hunting license, fish or game limits, or boat registration or area permit. Furthermore, such inspections may be made on a random basis, as long as they are not made in a discriminatory fashion. Evidence observed in plain view may be seized and used to support an arrest or warrant.

c. **Aircraft**: Aircraft should be treated in the same manner as boats and conventional vehicles. As with boats, airplanes may be boarded for safety inspections, and evidence observed in plain view may be seized and used to support an arrest or warrant.

An aircraft may be boarded without a warrant if there are exigent circumstances or probable cause that it contains evidence of a crime or violations of hunting or fishing limits.

6. **Protective sweeps**: Where there is a legitimate need to secure an area for such purposes as: public safety (e.g., bomb threat), dignitary protection, protection of officers conducting searches, prevention of the destruction of evidence, etc., you may perform a protective sweep of the area. Evidence discovered during the course of a proper sweep can be seized.

7. **Abandoned property**: Property that has been discarded may be searched without a warrant. This would include such things as: any property that is discarded by a suspect attempting to avoid discovery by law enforcement officers, thrown out the window of a vehicle or a room, left unattended in a public area for an extended period of time, remaining in a hotel room, dormitory room, or storage room after a person has checked out, etc.

Additionally, garbage placed for collection or discard at the point where the public or animals would have access to it is generally considered abandoned. For example, items in a garbage container placed for collection could be searched without a warrant.

8. **Border (international boundary) searches**: Individuals attempting to enter the United States at the border or when they land at airports are subject to a complete search of their person and all property in their possession.

CHAPTER 9
EVIDENCE

A. DEFINITION

Evidence is any form of proof, or probative matter, legally presented at a trial by the parties through the use of witnesses, records, documents, and concrete objects for the purpose of inducing belief in the minds of the court or jury. Evidence includes the presentation of any facts in a case that tend to either confirm or deny the truth of an assertion made by one of the parties in the case.

Evidence could also be of value for administrative hearings (e.g., disciplinary or termination hearings). When used for this purpose, the standards of evidence are generally not the same for administrative hearings as for judicial hearings.

What types of evidence are there?

Evidence may be either *direct* or *circumstantial*.

Direct evidence is any evidence that, in and of itself, tends to confirm an element or issue in question in the trial, without the need to produce other facts necessary to its introduction. An example would be eye witness testimony.

Circumstantial evidence is indirect evidence; that is, it involves facts from which the truth of an issue may be logically inferred. An example would be fingerprints on the murder weapon or testimony from a witness that he was in the area at the time the shot was heard and saw the defendant near the scene at about the time of the offense.

What are the different categories of evidence?

Evidence may be **testimonial**; that is, provided in the form of a testimony by a person, such as an eye witness or a person giving a confession.

Evidence may be **documentary**; that is, every form of writing, such as the guest register of a hotel or a shop keeper's financial records.

Evidence may be **real**; that is, all items directly involved in the incident such as blood stains, tire marks, powder burns, or a gun.

Demonstrative evidence is normally relevant and admissible if it demonstrates that the crime was committed and sheds some light on how it was committed. It includes weapons, blood-stained clothing, lifted fingerprints, photographs, mock-ups, models and similar items to aid in understanding the testimony.

Normally the conclusions or opinions of a witness are irrelevant and accordingly inadmissible. Qualified witnesses may render estimates or opinions of sobriety, age, race, speed, etc. Experts may testify and give professional opinions only in the area of their expertise, but they may not testify about common matters.

B. ADMISSIBILITY OF EVIDENCE

What is required to get evidence admitted at trial?

1. The evidence must be **relevant**; it must have some bearing on the facts at issue in the case. The question to ask is, does the evidence tend to prove or disprove the guilt of a person charged with a crime? As an example, evidence showing that a defendant owned a large mixed ring of General Motors keys may be relevant if the accused is charged with illegally entering General Motors vehicles and taking property from them.

2. The evidence must be **trustworthy**; it must be demonstrated that the evidence was not altered or tampered with. The *chain of custody* is an important means of preserving the integrity of the evidence as it is transferred from one person to another.

3.   The evidence must be **competent**; that is, it must have been obtained within the constitutional guidelines (most often the Fourth and Fifth Amendments), or it may be subject to suppression under the *Exclusionary Rule.*

Under what conditions may I legally obtain physical or documentary evidence of a crime?

a.   If you observe it in plain view when you had a legitimate right to be where you were when you saw it,

b.   if you have a valid warrant to search for it,

c.   if you have a valid consent to search for it,

d.   if you discover it during a search incident to a valid arrest,

e.   if someone willingly gives it to you,

f.   if you discover it on public or in abandoned property,

g.   if you find abandoned property that itself becomes evidence,

h.   if you discover it during a valid inventory of a vehicle or other item,

i.   if you inadvertently discover it during the course of a proper "Terry" frisk.

C. CHAIN OF CUSTODY

How do I protect the chain of custody?

To demonstrate the trustworthiness of any evidence you must be able to do the following two things:

1.   account for and document its whereabouts from the time you discovered it until it is entered at trial.

2. detail who had access to it from the time you discovered it until it is entered at trial.

For example, you seize a pound of marijuana that you discover in a vehicle you were searching incident to the arrest of its driver for selling drugs in a shopping center parking lot. You place the evidence in a sealed container and tag it with information regarding when, where, and from whom it was seized and who seized it. You then turn the evidence over to someone who is in charge of the locked property room, safe, or other system for storing evidence in a secure manner. Furthermore, you document the transfer on paper.

Similarly, any time the evidence is moved or changes hands it should be documented in writing, until it is finally admitted at trial. At no point in its "chain" should there be a possibility of tampering with or altering the evidence.

What if I intend to send evidence through the mail?

Any evidence sent through the mail should be sent "registered" which means that it travels in a secured way and must be signed for upon delivery. For example, you arrest a person for driving while intoxicated. The person submits to a blood alcohol test at the local hospital. At the hospital you witness the drawing of the sample, seal the container and mail it to a forensic laboratory for analysis. The package should be sent by "registered" mail. Unless the laboratory is familiar with procedures for handling evidence, you should request that it be returned by registered mail.

D. RULES OF EVIDENCE

What are the Rules of Evidence?

Both the federal and state court systems have written rules or guidelines that establish the admissibility of evidence at trial. These rules are actually rules of process or exclusion; they elaborate what will be acceptable and unacceptable as evidence, and how the evidence should be offered.

CHAPTER 10

TALKING WITH SUSPECTS

A. CONVENTIONAL CONVERSATION

Because of their unique role, it would not be considered inappropriate for police, for example, to casually approach some people on a sidewalk or in a corridor and make "small talk" with them. Nor would it be inappropriate on a deserted street after dark to approach an individual and ask if everything is alright. Such intrusions would not generally be considered unreasonable as long as they do not interfere with the individual's activities and are not intruding unnecessarily into his or her privacy.

Of course, this latitude given to you as a law enforcement officer works to your advantage when you are suspicious that criminal activity may be present. Because you may make such contacts legitimately, anything you may observe, hear, or smell of an illegal nature during such a contact would serve to help develop probable cause for further legal action. For example, you approach a parked car in the parking lot of a closed store at 3:00 AM to inquire whether the occupants are in need of assistance, and you see a "baggie" of what appears to be marijuana in plain view in the ashtray. You could confiscate the baggie and write a citation or make an arrest for the controlled substance.

B. Investigative Contacts

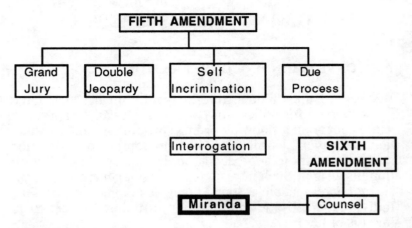

If you have reason to believe that a crime may have occurred and you are investigating the incident further, you have a right to ask questions of people whom you reasonably feel may have some knowledge of the incident. These people fall into two categories: (a) those who may have some information about the incident but are not suspects, and (b) those who may have some knowledge about the incident because they are suspects or potential suspects.

Furthermore, in this second group there are two subcategories: (1) those whom you have no intention of taking into physical custody and (2) those whom you may take into custody. It is important to remember that, for prosecutorial purposes, **no one** in any of the above categories is under any legal obligation to tell you **anything**.

If you plan to question a suspect, it is always wise to provide him or her with the "Miranda" warnings. It is **necessary** to provide the suspect with "Miranda" warnings if you take him or her into custody and are going to interrogate that person.

Yes. You may observe all activity you can see (including use of binoculars or scopes) and use the observation to support a warrant or effect an arrest. You may use a recording device (e.g., recording from the vehicle) to record any overheard remarks to support a warrant or effect an arrest.

May I wire another person and record the conversations in which he or she engages?

Yes. You may use recording or transmitting devices placed on another person to transmit all conversations of people talking with the wired individual. The court will allow this as being more accurate than testimony of the wired person. You may not, however, place a microphone near a vehicle, phone booth, etc. without the necessary warrant. You could, however, set up a recording device in a nearby vehicle or area and record all sounds naturally coming to the site.

May I listen in on an extension phone to a conversation?

Yes. You may listen in if you have the consent of any of the parties in the conversation. If you do not have the consent of at least one of the parties, you may not listen in without a warrant.

Do I need a warrant to listen to conversations in a motel room or apartment?

You should have a warrant to listen to sounds because the occupants have a reasonable expectation of privacy. You may observe from a public or adjoining area all activity around you and use that or any sounds heard by the unaided ear to support an arrest or warrant.

What if I hear a scream or shot?

You may respond as in any exigent circumstance and enter the premises to insure the safety of others.

Where do I get the sound surveillance warrant?

You should contact your prosecutor to assist you in obtaining the warrant.

B. INFORMANTS

Informants may be used to support search or arrest warrants and, under appropriate circumstances, warrantless arrests. You may stop individuals pursuant to an informant's information to determine the presence of criminal activity.

Informants should be reliable; that is, the information, coupled with past reliability of the informant or other corroborating circumstances, would lead a reasonable police officer acting in good faith to believe that sufficient probable cause exists to proceed with an arrest or seek a warrant. You should obtain information pertaining to the identity of your informant so your can corroborate the basis of your probable cause at a later time.

If, for example, a person in a mall parking lot tells me that the individual in the next vehicle has a weapon in his or her waistband and is selling cocaine from a briefcase, what may I do?

You may **stop** the individual, reach into the waistband (frisk), take the weapon, and, based on that (corroboration), open the briefcase and effect the arrest.

C. OPEN FIELDS

Open fields are the areas outside of occupied premises, and the area immediately around such, including most public space, where a police officer may go freely. You may observe and listen from these areas and use such observations to effect an arrest or support a warrant.

D. PLAIN VIEW

Any evidence, fruits, or instrumentalities of a crime that you observe without your having to move anything, turn any-

3. Nudity: Expression has on occasion taken the form of nudity. The use of nudity as expression may be limited to those demonstrations of value, such as a play, and even then it may be limited to a reasonable display. It is possible not to be obscene in the use of nudity. However, nudity, simply for nudity's sake, is not within the protection of the Constitution and may be banned from public areas. Nudity may be protected in places of entertainment, depending upon local ordinances.

Does presence at a public place like a park, coliseum, stadium, or parking lot affect free speech or free expression?

First, it must be determined if the location and nature of expression is relevant in terms of time, place and subject of the protest. Generally, protests not identified with an institution may be restricted or prohibited. As an example, a sit-in on the city hall steps to protest a local tax increase may be acceptable, but a protest against a national tax increase may not. A protest blocking access to a clinic probably would not be warranted, but a similar protest in front of an administration building or public square concerning a controversial speaker may be. A protest on the public street in front of the fire station concerning lack of adequate funds for fire services may be acceptable, whereas any protest interfering with fire department responses should not be tolerated.

B. FREEDOM OF THE PRESS

Freedom of the press is very similar to speech. Distribution of handbills, papers, etc. may not be halted in public areas as a general rule. Persons do not have to accept the material, however, and individuals littering may be cited or arrested for such activity, but not for the distribution of the material, *per se.*

C. FREEDOM OF RELIGION

Religious services may be conducted on public property so long as they are not dangerous to the participants or others, not unnecessarily intrusive or imposing on others, and within the constraints of the property's usage. As an example, a religious service may be conducted in the public square or mall, even if the religion is not conventional. There is no right to compel others to hear or participate in the activities, however, or to use regularly restricted areas. For example, if an area of the mall or auditorium is closed at midnight, a religious group would not necessarily have a right to enter the closed area for services, without special permission.

D. OFFICIAL ACTION

The notion that certain groups are not "using a public place for its intended purpose" and, therefore, should be removed and kept from interfering with the *bona fide* users is beginning to lose favor with the courts. A balancing of the right of privacy and public use versus compelling state interests seems to be the courts' stance.

As a general rule you, as a police officer, should not deny non-traditional groups the use of public areas if their activities do not truly represent a threat or significant impediment to necessary operations or persons' freedom.

For example, if a group requests a permit to hold a demonstration against the government's policies toward nuclear arms, such a request should not be denied out of hand because it is not in keeping with the "intended purpose." You may, however, be able to restrict some areas and activities for reasons of area protection. As an example, you may keep the demonstrators out of a recently sodded grassy area to give the grass a chance to grow. You could not, however, exclude the group as individuals from entering an area, provided they meet appropriate regulations or requirements.

behavior or refuses to make the group conform to appropriate conduct. The juveniles could, of course, be taken into custody for their conduct.

Likewise, in most jurisdictions a non-spouse adult who is engaging in sexual activity with a juvenile is contributing to the juvenile's delinquency.

6. Stopping juveniles:

When I stop a vehicle containing several youths and ask them to empty their pockets and they flee, may I take them into custody?

Yes. The flight under those circumstances is adequate probable cause to take them into custody.

If I approach a group of young people on a street corner and ask if they are having fun and they run, is that adequate probable cause?

No, not without other factors or observations. It would, however, justify a stop and, if warranted, a frisk.

May I ask juveniles found in a public bathroom what they are doing?

Yes, particularly if there are any supporting circumstances such as smoke, beer cans, liquor bottles, a noisy crowd, etc.

If I see several youths drinking beer may I ask for their identifications?

Yes. You may ask for the identification and follow up with more inquiry of those without proper identification or those under the drinking age. The people should be able to prove that they are adults, unless it is apparent.

May I detain a youthful suspect?

You may detain a youthful suspect more easily than an adult if you have the requisite reasonable suspicion, but you must act more quickly to secure a detention hearing and keep the youth segregated from adults during the detention.

7. **Custody disputes involving juveniles:** You should have written policy and procedures concerning juveniles and their custody. That policy and procedure should be coordinated with the local juvenile authorities and court.

Generally disputes over custody of a juvenile occur when one parent has legitimate custody and the other does not. In these situations, the parent with legitimate custody and necessary documents to prove such should be allowed actual or temporary custody of any juveniles in the dispute. When conflict arises because of a dispute over custody, regardless of the reasons or the presence of conflicting documents, the juvenile should be placed in the custody of the local juvenile court for a determination of custody, and the resultant court order should be followed. While you may have ample evidence to determine disposition, you do not have to make the determination yourself.

If there is a dispute with an alien or there is a matter of international consequence, the juvenile should be taken into custody, immediately transported to the *local* juvenile court, and the matter referred to the court for disposition.

If a juvenile is alone and becomes confused, disoriented, lost, appears to be a runaway, or is being transported for placement or disposition under the Interstate Compact concerning juveniles, the juvenile should be taken into custody and transported to the local juvenile court or authorities for disposition. Temporarily lost juveniles should, of course, be returned to their parents or guardians unless there is a dispute in any form, in which case the matter should be referred to the local juvenile authorities.

If a parent approaches you and says, "My spouse is kidnapping my child," what may I do?

You may intercept the parent with the child and inquire into the circumstances. If there is any conflict which cannot be easily resolved, the juvenile should be taken into custody, and the matter should be referred to the local juvenile authorities or court. This is particularly true if the parent with the child is in the process of traveling. In that instance the local court should determine the right of custody.

If I find a young child who is lost and wandering around, what may I do?

After a brief, thorough check for parents or guardians, the juvenile should be transported to local authorities for disposition. You should not turn the child over to anyone who cannot prove his or her right of custody. For example, an aunt should be readily identifiable by discussion with the child, the parents on the phone, general information, etc. before the child is permitted to go with her. Do not release the juvenile to some stranger willing to help.

C. DEALING WITH MILITARY PERSONNEL

1. Members of the American Armed Forces

Police are often faced with having to take law enforcement action against someone who is a member of the American Armed Forces. It is important to know that these situations often necessitate special procedures. It is possible that you would not know that a person was in the military, in which instance you should proceed as you would in any other situation. If it becomes apparent to you that a person is in the military, you should proceed as noted below.

May I write a member of the Armed Services a citation?

Yes, if you encounter a person engaging in an act for which you would normally write a citation, even if he or she is on active duty with some branch of the Armed Services, you may write the citation.

May I give a member of the Armed Services a summons to court to answer for violating a law or regulation which I have authority to enforce?

Yes, if you would normally give a summons to an individual for committing the offense, you may give the summons to the member of the Armed Services.

May I arrest a member of the Armed Services?

Yes. As an example, you work in an area near an army base, and you apprehend an off-duty soldier for driving while intoxicated. He tells you that he has to be back at the base in half an hour. You may arrest the individual as you would anyone else.

Once I arrest a member of the Armed Services, is the judicial process any different from what it would be for anyone else?

No. The judicial process for arrest, detention, providing constitutional rights, or care is no different in so far as your actions are concerned. There may, however, be a different process for the military person in the system. If the matter is merely a citation and it is resolved, the matter should be considered closed. If, however, circumstances, either because of impact or seriousness, warrant further action the nearest appropriate prosecutor's office and the nearest military installation (air police, military police or shore patrol) should be notified, giving the charges, name, rank, serial number, military organization, if known, and installation.

2. Members of foreign armed forces

Should members of foreign armed forces be treated any differently from members of the American Armed Forces?

No. You should, however, notify the United States Attorney's Office or the United States Department of State of the arrest, including the charges, name, rank and serial number. For example, a foreign navy vessel is moored in a harbor nearby, and you apprehend several sailors on shore leave selling cocaine. They should be arrested and the procedures followed as previously noted.

D. Establishing Probable Cause With Intoxicated Drivers

With respect to the public's safety, one of the most important enforcement functions you serve is to detect and apprehend people who are driving under the influence of drugs or alcohol. In order to arrest a person for driving under the influence (D.U.I.) and have the person's blood or breath analyzed for the presence of alcohol, you must first establish probable cause that the person is, indeed, D.U.I. In some jurisdictions this is still a relatively easy matter, but because the nation's laws against drunk driving are becoming more punitive, there is also an increasing sophistication among defense attorneys that enables them to more competently discredit you or your testimony when a D.U.I. case reaches trial. In order to present a good case against a drunk driver, it is necessary that you be systematic and thorough in your development of probable cause and in the documentation of your case. Although each court may be different, there are some general guidelines which, if followed, will make it much more difficult for a defense attorney to win a D.U.I. case for his or her client. The following guidelines are presented to help you develop probable cause in a D.U.I. case and then not lose the case when you go to court.

Before you can have a blood or breath test administered to a suspected D.U.I., you must have probable cause that he or she is D.U.I. and effect an arrest based upon your probable cause. You establish your probable cause by observing (1) the suspect's driving behavior, (2) other driver behaviors during your traffic stop, and (3) the driver's performance on selected field sobriety tests.

What are some kinds of initial observations of driver behavior that may be used to raise my suspicions that someone is driving under the influence?

a. weaving or crossing the center line several times,
b. straddling the center line,
c. driving considerably below the speed limit,
d. failing to dim headlights to oncoming traffic,
e. speeding,

f. ignoring traffic signals or signs,
g. littering,
h. excessive use of brakes,
i. turning with a wide radius,
j. following too closely,
k. almost striking another vehicle or object,
l. driving off designated roadways.

During my stop of a potential D.U.I. offender, what types of observations might increase my suspicions?

a. delayed stopping response to your emergency lights or siren,
b. excessive movement of occupants in vehicle,
c. partial roll-down of driver's window,
d. red, watery, or glassy eyes,
e. flushed face,
f. slow or slurred speech,
g. odor of intoxicating beverage (alcohol itself does not have an odor),
h. fumbling in wallet for operator's license,
i. presence of alcoholic beverages in vehicle,
j. delays in responding to requests (e.g., to turn down volume on radio, to provide operator's license or vehicle registration, etc.),
k. excessive belligerence,
l. driver sick or vomiting.

If I suspect that a driver may be under the influence and I attempt to remove him or her from the vehicle, what else should I look for?

a. awkward or unsteady gait,
b. attempts to lean on vehicle for support,
c. difficulty maintaining balance while exiting vehicle,
d. difficulty maintaining balance while standing,
e. indications of stomach sickness, vomiting, etc.

If I continue to suspect D.U.I. and want to administer field sobriety tests, what points are relevant to developing probable cause for an arrest?

1. Before using any field sobriety tests, you should (a) be trained in their administration by an expert, and (b) have an opportunity to practice executing them and administering them. Remember, you will probably be asked to demonstrate these tests in court.

2. Demonstrate each test you plan to administer just prior to administering it.

3. Administer more than one test (at least three would be preferable).

4. If driver fails any test, give him or her at least two more chances to perform it.

5. Record the order of tests given.

6. Record the number of attempts that driver made to pass each test.

7. Record the specific way in which driver failed each test.

8. Remember to make note of any statements the driver may make about speech impediments, inner ear infections, medication, or other conditions that may affect his or her balance or test performance.

What are some of the generally accepted field sobriety tests?

Several different types of tests have been developed and, before deciding on the ones you will use, it is a good idea to find out which ones are preferred by the prosecutors and judges who may be dealing with your D.U.I. cases. Below is a list of some of the more commonly accepted field sobriety tests:

1. Tests of balance:

a.   one leg stand test: driver stands on one leg, holds other leg straight out in front, about six inches off the ground for 30 seconds (driver counts slowly to 30 while looking at the raised foot),

b.   heel-to-toe test: driver walks a real or imaginary straight line heel-to-toe for nine steps, pivots slowly on the left foot, and walks back nine steps; driver counts the steps out loud and watches his or her feet while walking,

c.   heel-to-toe/pick-up-coin test: driver walks heel-to-toe for about nine steps, bends over to pick up a coin from the ground, and then stands up straight,

2.   Tests of coordination: Finger-to-nose test: driver shuts eyes, tips head back, extends arms out to side and then attempts to touch nose by first placing the index finger of one hand then the index finger of the other, on nose.

3.   Tests involving speech:

a.   recite the complete alphabet, preferably by beginning with some letter in the middle such as "G".

b.   counting-fingers test: Using one hand only, driver counts fingers while simultaneously touching thumb to the four fingers, beginning with the little finger, going to the index, and then counts backwards beginning with the index and going to the little finger. Thus, the counting sequence is "one, two, three, four, four, three, two, one," and the appropriate fingers must be touched. When driver finishes with one hand, he or she then counts fingers on other hand in same manner.

4.   Horizontal gaze nystagmus test: This test is based on the fact that alcohol impairment usually affects the eyes' ability to efficiently follow objects moving back and forth in a horizontal plane. The driver is asked to hold his or her head still while visually following a moving object (e.g., a pen) as the officer moves it back and forth in front of the driver's face.

What information should be included in the incident report that I will take to court?

In addition to the standard information, you should include the following:

1. your initial observations that led you to make the traffic stop,

2. any significant observations about how the violator responded to your request to "pull over,"

3. any relevant observations about the violator's physical and verbal behavior, odors, liquor in the vehicle, etc. when you first made contact,

4. any relevant observations about how the violator acted or what the violator said when he or she exited the vehicle,

5. what field sobriety tests you administered, the order in which they were given, how many times each was attempted, whether they were passed or failed and, if they were failed, in what specific ways they were failed,

6. any other observations about the violator's behavior that may be relevant, e.g., general demeanor, vomiting, belligerence, statements about drinking, etc.

What if a suspected D.U.I. refuses to take a field sobriety or a blood or breath test?

Most states have "implied consent" laws which means that a refusal to take the test results in loss of driving privileges for a certain period of time. However, it is important to remember that you may be able to successfully prosecute a D.U.I. case based upon your general observations of the driver's behavior before and during the traffic stop as well as on other evidence that may be available (e.g., open liquor bottles). In other words, in the case of uncooperative drivers, the results of field sobriety tests or blood or breath samples are not necessarily required for conviction. Clearly, in such cases, as well as all D.U.I. cases, the quality of your observations and report will be critical.

E. MODEL INVENTORY POLICY

It shall be the policy of _____ to inventory all private or abandoned property that is impounded, regardless of reason. This policy is to be followed in its entirety by all personnel. The purpose of the inventory procedure is to protect any valuable property that may be part of an impoundment and protect the institution from the possibility of negligence in the loss of private property. The inventory procedure is **not** to be used as an alternative to obtaining a search warrant in those cases in which it is suspected that evidence of criminal activity may be present with the impounded property.

Inventorying impounded vehicles: When any vehicle is impounded by police, it will be completely inventoried and will include the passenger compartment, the glove box, the trunk, the spare tire well, ashtrays, and any unlocked or unsealed containers, regardless of size. Examples of containers would include, but are not limited to, such things as: backpacks, handbags, purses, film canisters, flashlights, wallets, picnic baskets, athletic bags, camera cases, glasses cases, diaper bags, luggage of all types, tool boxes and kits, first aid kits, plastic or paper bags, tackle boxes, shoes, boots, rifle and pistol cases, cardboard boxes, etc. Any containers that are locked or sealed (e.g., with strapping tape) should normally be inventoried as single units, without opening them. If you have reason to believe, more than mere suspicion, that the item contains evidence, fruits or instrumentalities of a crime, you may open the container. However, you would be better advised to obtain a warrant. If you have articulable suspicion that an item contains dangerous materials you may, because of public safety, open the container. Wheel covers and hubcaps will be removed and placed in the trunk to secure them. The engine area will be checked for anything of special value (e.g., chrome parts).

When the inventory is complete, all items of value will be secured, and a written record of everything of value will be made and signed by the inventorying officer(s).

110

Inventorying non-vehicles: In the event that other property is impounded (e.g., camera equipment, backpacks, handbags, briefcases, etc.), a complete inventory will be made and will include inventorying all unlocked or unsealed containers. Each locked or sealed container should be inventoried as a single unit without opening it.

When the inventory is complete, all items of value will be secured, and a written record of everything of value will be made and signed by the inventorying officer(s). All property found and in custody of the police department that was not obtained pursuant to a seizure will be inventoried.

Evidence: If, during the inventory procedure, evidence or fruits or instrumentalities of a crime should be inadvertently discovered, the inventorying officer(s) shall stop the inventory immediately, secure the property being inventoried, maintain the chain of custody of the found evidence, and notify supervisory personnel. The purpose for this procedure is to allow a decision to be made as to whether to seek a warrant to search the impounded vehicle or property.

F. DIPLOMATIC IMMUNITY

Persons whom you have detained for committing violations of regulations or committing crimes and who claim diplomatic immunity may be held to verify their diplomatic status. In such cases it is your responsibility to immediately contact the United States Department of State to verify their claim. Follow the instructions of the appropriate State Department authority. During this time treat the individual(s) with respect and care and do not conduct a search of their persons or property. You may, of course, frisk to protect yourself or others, if warranted. You should also notify the United States or State's Attorney of the person's identity and the offense. If the matter is minor, you should consult your supervisor. The person with diplomatic immunity may be merely cited or expelled from a particular place and the same authorities notified.

G. Use of Dogs

Although dogs are becoming increasingly valuable as a law enforcement tool, their use expands the officer's exposure to liability. For this reason dogs should always be under the handler's complete control.

In a search situation, does a trained dog's alert to objects such as firearms or drugs constitute probable cause for an arrest or seizure?

As with all probable cause situations, it would depend upon the totality of the circumstances. Included would be such elements as: appropriate training on the part of the dog and handler, evidence of the dog's reliability, appropriate alerting behavior, and whether the officer and dog have a right to be where they are at the search time.

What are the issues surrounding the use of dogs and excessive force?

Two areas should be considered: apprehending a suspect and crowd control. When apprehending a suspect, the dog may be used to assist in locating, subduing, and bringing the suspect into custody. Care must be exercised that any force exerted by the dog is not excessive, as the dog is an extension of the officer. Simply stated, if the dog uses excessive force, the officer may be liable. In the case of crowd control, the dog may be used defensively to hold a crowd at bay or move it. However, extreme care must be taken that the dog does not become an agent of excessive force, i.e., be allowed to bite someone who is not assaulting the dog or handler.

H. Special Law Enforcement Incidents

Some law enforcement agencies have developed S.W.A.T. teams to handle special situations requiring heavy law enforcement intervention. To avoid potential exposure to liability for negligent activities related to the management of such incidents, the skill and training level which the team brings to an incident must be at least equal to that possessed by other area teams that could otherwise be called to handle the situation. The underlying rule is that the department may not deprive the public of the best available policing techniques and skills.

In any case, law enforcement officers not trained in S.W.A.T. tactics should never function as S.W.A.T. team members. Furthermore, all S.W.A.T. activities, including training, should be driven by written policy and procedure.

Law enforcement management must operate with an awareness that S.W.A.T. teams may tend to over respond because of the exigencies of the crisis. Thus, management should carefully temper any response in these situations.

Of course, the same requirements would hold for a police department's involvement in hostage negotiations, handling bomb threats, dignitary protection, etc. This would include the requirement for written policies and procedures.

In any bomb threat situation, unless you are absolutely sure that the bomb does not exist, individuals in the area should be immediately evacuated to safety before any other action occurs.

NOTES

CHAPTER 15

AN OVERVIEW OF LIABILITY

Concern over liability issues has been the driving force behind major changes in law enforcement procedures, selection standards, training, deployment, supervision and retention. In fact, it is fair to say that it has been the primary driving force behind law enforcement reform in general. In spite of its importance, however, many law enforcement practitioners are relatively unaware of the nature of liability and liability exposure and how these concepts impact the law enforcement function in institutional settings. What follows is a review of these concepts and the categories of liability.

What is legal liability?

Legal liability is the responsibility a person has under law for his or her actions or inactions.

What is legal duty?

Legal duty can be defined as that which a person is legally obligated to do or refrain from doing. Generally, a person has a duty to exercise reasonable care to avoid subjecting other persons or their property to unreasonable risks of harm.

Legal duty may also be that which one should do, based on the probability or foreseeability of injury to a party. As public servants, police officers have imposed on them a duty that they must meet for ethical and professional reasons. Carrying out this legal duty will also reduce their exposure to liability.

What is the "public duty doctrine"?

The "public duty doctrine" refers to a duty owed by a law enforcement officer to the public, as a whole, to provide for the general safety and welfare; it is not owed to any particular individual as such. As an example, police have a general duty to remove drunk drivers from roads.

What is a "special duty" owed to an individual?

A "special duty" is a duty owed to a particular individual or
class of individuals that results from a special relationship.
For example, there is a special duty incumbent on an officer
to remove a person incapacitated in the middle of a roadway
to a place of safety. The special duty is imposed on the officer because of the duty and the resultant training and skills to
provide for safety for those unable to secure their own.

In a civil lawsuit what options for obtaining relief are open to the plaintiff?

a.   *Injunction*: the plaintiff may sue to have the defendant
     cease an action.

b.   *Commence action*: the plaintiff may also sue to have the
     defendant begin an action (e.g., put up a fence).

c.   *Damages*: the plaintiff may sue to obtain a monetary
     judgment from the defendant to "balance the wrong" of
     some act. *Direct damages* cover direct losses as a result
     of the negligent act and compensation for such things as
     pain and suffering. *Punitive damages* are sometimes
     awarded in addition to direct damages as a "fine" the de-
     fendant has to pay to the plaintiff as a result of some
     grossly negligent, willful, or reckless act that inflicted
     the loss or injury.

What are the various categories of liability, and how are they defined?

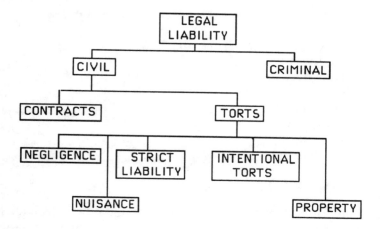

Legal liability may be divided into two main categories: *criminal* and *civil.*

Criminal Liability: Criminal liability is the culpability or responsibility for an act or failure to act that has been defined by law as a harm against the state. The violation of criminal laws amounts to an act against the state (as well as the person who was the actual victim of the act). In other words, in criminal liability, it is the state (public as a whole) which has been wronged.

Civil Liability: Civil liability is the culpability or responsibility for an act or failure to act that caused a loss or harm to another individual, but is not considered to be a wrong against the state.

What are the categories of civil liability?

There are two principal types of civil liability:

a.　Liability involving **contracts.**
b.　Liability involving **torts.** This category would be of most interest to those in policing.

What is a tort?

A **tort** may be thought of as a loss or a harm sustained by a person that supports the legal basis for a lawsuit.

Are there different types of torts?

Yes. Torts may be divided into the following types:
a. Negligence
b. Strict liability
c. Intentional torts
d. Nuisance
e. Property torts

What is "liability" in tort law?

Liability in tort law is a creation of individual case decisions, commonly referred to as the common law. Generally, conduct may be tortuous only if there is a legal duty to act or avoid an act, which results in injury. No jurisdiction has attempted to completely codify this area of law. Accordingly, when we talk about tort law we do so without definition; we are, nonetheless, seeking principles and rules to avoid liability.

Perhaps the easiest way to understand this law is to recognize that it is a part of civil law, i.e., it is concerned with what the individual can do to find remedy for an injury sustained from the action or inaction of another party. Remember, however, that a civil wrong may also be a criminal wrong and, therefore, punishable by the state.

What is the purpose of tort law?

There are three purposes in this area of law:
1. Compensate the victim: in so far as possible to "make whole" the victim, as much as the money paid in damages can.
2. Provide justice: by requiring those responsible to pay the determined damages.
3. Deter others: society is made safer by deterring dangerous behavior which creates injury.

What is required to demonstrate tort liability?

Liability requires the following four elements:
1. A **duty** owed to the injured party by the party responsible for the injury.
2. A **breach** of that duty because of the action or inaction of the party responsible for the injury.
3. An **injury** to the party to whom the duty was owed.
4. A **causal connection** between 2 and 3 above.

What is meant by "proximate cause"?

Proximate cause is a legal fiction used to limit a defendant's liability. It requires that the injury has a reasonable relationship to the tortious conduct. As a rule, one must consider whether the consequences of the act were foreseeable and whether or not intervening causes exist. Normally, liability is limited to individuals who were in the foreseeable area of hazard and where the foreseeability was present when the injury took place.

A defendant, therefore, may be liable if he or she could have foreseen any harm from his or her actions or lack thereof. Furthermore, the defendant may be liable even if it was not foreseeable, unless the court finds that the likelihood that the conduct would cause the resultant harm was too remote or unusual.

NOTES

CHAPTER 16

TORT LIABILITY: NEGLIGENCE

What are the different types of torts?

The categories of torts include negligence, nuisance, strict liability, intentional torts and property.

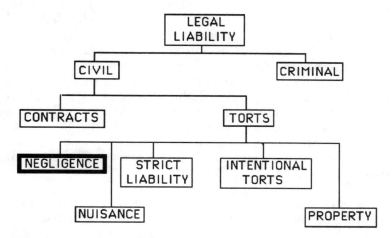

What is Negligence?

Negligence is an act or failure to act that results in loss or injury to an innocent party. Negligence is conduct (whether intentional or not) that fails to conform to legal standards. A jury normally makes a determination of negligence by asking whether a defendant's conduct was the same as the fictional "reasonably prudent person," placed in the same circumstances.

Must I be perfect?

The law requires no one to be perfect but only that he or she act as the reasonably prudent person would in a similar situation. The reasonably prudent person is a legal fiction, but generally is perceived as one with normal or average attributes. However, in cases in which people must possess

121

more knowledge or higher qualifications, skills, or intellect than the average reasonably prudent person, they may be held to the higher level. Law enforcement officers would fall into such a category, and they must exhibit the appropriate standard of care.

What is meant by "standard of care"?

Standard of care (in negligence cases) represents the level of care a reasonable person of similar skills and qualifications would use under similar circumstances. It is the criterion by which courts evaluate behavior—the fictional "reasonable person." The resultant standard of care is normally couched in terms of "ordinary care," "due care," or "reasonable care." Implicit in this legal doctrine is the notion that the standard of reasonableness is not normally met if a person engages in an act or failure to act that results in an injury or loss to someone else. Reasonableness implies that if the person either *knew or should have known* that his or her behavior could be the proximate cause of injury to another, and an injury occurs, then an acceptable standard of care is not met.

Thus, a defendant's liability for an injury is founded upon what he or she knew or should have known of a risk, and that a sufficient degree of probability is present that will cause a harm to a plaintiff. An officer must understand the parameters of reasonableness as applicable to his or her duties under the law. No provision is made for any weaknesses of an officer, so any forgetful, careless, ignorant, foolish, rash, impetuous, timid, or clumsy person is held to the "reasonable person" standard whether he or she can conform or not.

How are standards of care established?

Standards of care are often created by case law, guidelines for juries, legislative histories, legislation, and rules of law, but are generally left to juries. Generally, the violation of a law (statute) is negligence *per se*, which means that if the defendant fails to introduce evidence which excuses the violation, the negligence as to the defendant is conclusively established.

122

NOTES

CHAPTER 17

TORT LIABILITY:
STRICT LIABILITY, INTENTIONAL
TORTS, AND NUISANCE

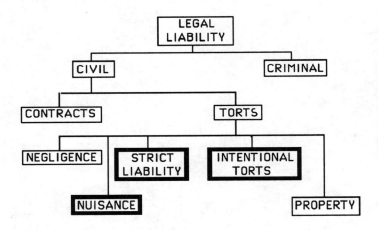

A. STRICT LIABILITY

What is strict liability?

Strict liability refers to situations in which a person may be held liable even though the person exhibited reasonable care and did nothing "wrong." Having to "make good" on a product that turned out to be defective would be an example of strict liability.

While strict liability may be imposed in other areas, in a public institution it is routinely associated with abnormally dangerous activity. Factors that may be associated with the rule are:

1.   What is the extent of risk? That is, how high a degree of risk of harm exists, and what is the likelihood that the harm to others will be great?

2. Is there an ability to eliminate the risk? If the risk remains after reasonable care is taken to avoid it, the possibility of strict liability may still exist.

3. Is it an abnormal activity? The further away from common usage, the greater the exposure to strict liability.

4. Location: Is the activity being conducted in an improper place?

5. Societal interests: Does the activity's value exceed its social value?

What are some limitations on strict liability?

a. Proximate cause requires the harm to result from the abnormal danger for liability to be established.

b. Legislative action may preclude strict liability, or legislation authorizing one to carry on the activity will normally exclude strict liability. Legislation may also create strict liability in certain situations.

B. INTENTIONAL TORT

What is an intentional tort?

An **intentional tort** occurs when the loss or harm caused by the action or inaction was intended by the person inflicting the tort.

What is intent?

Intent is a desire to cause a particular consequence by a specific act or the belief that the end result is a substantial certainty of the act.

Examples of Intentional Torts

What is a battery?

Battery is offensive physical contact with another or with something in his or her immediate control or possession. Something as simple as knocking off a hat could be a battery.

What is assault?

If a person intentionally places another in apprehension of an imminent battery, an **assault** has occurred. There must be an intent to cause the contact; the plaintiff must be aware (apprehension) of the act before its termination; and there must be an apparent intent and ability to carry out the threat at that time.

As an example, a person firing a weapon at another, but missing, does not commit an assault (civil) unless the person at whom the shot was directed is aware of the incident and, therefore, apprehensive of the shot. This is distinguished from criminal assault, which does not require knowledge or apprehension on the part of the intended victim, because the action is viewed as being against the public as a whole. Furthermore, assault requires that no privilege to use force exists. For example, a police officer physically expelling a rowdy party from a public establishment would not generally be liable for an assault.

What is false imprisonment?

The intentional confinement of a person by an individual, absent legal authority, is **false imprisonment**. As an example, the detention by a law enforcement officer of an individual for shoplifting could be false imprisonment, absent probable cause for arrest or statutory relief permitting a brief detention for investigation.

What is intentional or reckless infliction of emotional distress?

A defendant is subject to liability to a plaintiff for **emotional distress**, or resulting harm, that is caused by extreme and outrageous behavior he or she intentionally performed. Abuse of power by a law enforcement officer which exceeds the ordinary means of persuasion or demand is designated as a flagrant abuse of power in the nature of extortion and, as such, may be actionable.

What are the defenses to liability for intentional torts?

a. *Privilege*: As a rule, privilege is created by consent or an act of law, irrespective of consent. For example, a police officer is privileged to use reasonable force to apprehend an individual.

b. *Consent*: When one is willing for the conduct to occur, there is consent which is almost always a defense to any tort. For example, a person consents to battery in a football game, but this does not extend to excessive force which would exceed the consent.

c. *Self defense and defense of others*: A person is normally privileged to use reasonable force as is necessary to protect himself or herself from immediate physical harm threatened by the intentional or negligent conduct of another person. This includes the use of self defense against an assault, false imprisonment, or a negligently caused harm. Excessive force is not permitted, and any force used after the person extending the original conduct is subdued, disarmed, helpless, or has withdrawn from the fracas is not permitted.

Likewise, force may be utilized to come to the defense of another under the same circumstances that the third party would be privileged to defend him- or herself against. However, if the intervening defender is wrong, that mistake, no matter how reasonable, is irrelevant, and the defender may be liable for assault, battery, etc.

131

A person with a duty to protect another person or his or her property is privileged, under law, to use reasonable force or confinement, appropriate to the occasion, to effect the duty.

d. *Defending and recovering property*: One in possession of property may utilize reasonable force to expel another from or prevent trespass on property or prevent the taking of personal property. This is true even though the force used would normally be an assault, battery, or false imprisonment. Only necessary force is permitted, and any force likely to cause death or great bodily harm is not permitted.

One may use limited self-help to recapture one's property wrongfully and forcibly taken from one's possession, even where there is a claim of right, or if obtained by fraud or duress. The effort to recapture the property must begin immediately upon the dispossession or after learning of it so that it is a continuous, uninterrupted act. Demand to return the property must be made first. Then, if the demand is futile, only reasonable force, not force likely to cause serious bodily harm, may be used. Mistake as to the need for the force is no defense to liability.

e. *Necessity*: The defense of necessity may be used when defending one's person or property from some harm in a manner that results in harm to the plaintiff. Public necessity will be the defense which a law enforcement officer would most often use. For example, a police officer sets up a roadblock to stop a fleeing vehicle, and the vehicle swerves to miss the obstruction and runs into another's house. The officer's behavior would normally be excused so long as the reasonable care standard is met. The danger requiring the establishment of the roadblock affects the community as a whole, so that public interest is involved and, therefore, the privilege is allowed.

f. *Authority of law*: Individuals acting under the authority of law are privileged, under appropriate circumstances

132

to commit acts that would normally be assault, battery, imprisonment, and trespass. A law enforcement officer could, therefore, physically restrain (battery) an individual, handcuff him or her (confinement), and transport the person to the station, if it is in furtherance of reasonable law enforcement.

Ministerial v. discretionary acts: A law enforcement officer, using appropriate discretion, may in good faith determine how to act (e.g., whether to arrest or close off a street) and is privileged so to do. Ministerial (obligatory) acts, on the other hand, are not in the privileged category, regardless of good faith, if done improperly.

C. NUISANCE

What is an action for nuisance?

Nuisance refers to conduct, and generally is identified as either *public* or *private*. Private nuisance, a particular activity or thing which unreasonably and substantially interferes with a person's enjoyment of property, is normally of little consideration in public institutional settings. Public nuisance, on the other hand, is an unreasonable interference with a common collective right. Generally, this includes interference with public peace and safety, health and comfort, and public morals. These rights must be common to the public.

NOTES

CHAPTER 18

TORT LIABILITY:
OTHER LIABILITY CONSIDERATIONS

A. LIABILITY CONSIDERATIONS FOR EMPLOYERS AND EMPLOYEES

Does the employer-employee relationship generate any special concerns?

The employer-employee relationship creates liability for and toward one another.

1. *Vicarious liability*: An employer may be vicariously liable for the acts of his or her employee if the employee was acting within the scope of his or her employment. As noted previously, the department and supervisors most often will be placed in a position of liability for the acts of officers if the officers are acting within the color of law. The scope of employment factor is a question for the jury and they may take into consideration any factors having a bearing on the employment relationship.

2. *Intentional torts*: If an employee is acting within the scope of his or her employment, and intentionally commits a tortious act in furtherance of the employment, the employer is vicariously liable. Where there is a special duty of protection between an employer and a plaintiff, the employer may be vicariously liable for an injury in breach of that duty, whether committed in furtherance of the employer's interest or for personal reasons. For example, if an officer on routine patrol drives by and ignores a serious motor vehicle accident, or does not intervene when a fellow officer is using excessive force, the employer inherits the responsibility.

135

3. *Direct liability*: The employer may be directly liable, not vicariously liable, for the conduct of the employee. Most often the employer may be directly liable for such acts on his or her part in selecting, hiring, training, instructing, testing, supervising, evaluating, retraining, reassignment, etc. The employer may also be directly liable for the consequences of commanding or authorizing an employee's act.

In general, to escape liability, employers must provide a safe place to work with safe equipment or tools adequate for the job, with adequate competent fellow employees, under adequate supervision, and with training necessary to accomplish the work.

B. LIABILITY AND CONTRACTORS

How does the use of independent contractors affect liability exposure?

As a rule, an employer is not vicariously liable for physical harm caused by an independent contractor or its employees. However, there are exceptions to this rule, which include such things as: negligence standards and contract minimums, selection, instruction, failure to inspect and monitor work, retention of control and supervision, and duties of special relationships.

C. LIABILITY INVOLVING INTERFERENCE WITH FEDERAL CONSTITUTIONAL RIGHTS

Persons interfering with another's constitutional rights under color of law may be sued under 42 U.S.C. § 1983. (See Chapter 2 section on Civil Liability).

D. MISREPRESENTATION AND DEFAMATION

What is negligent misrepresentation?

An erroneous misrepresentation about another, even if honestly believed to be true, is actionable if it fails to meet professional or business standards, and there is a failure to exercise reasonable care in determining the truth.

What is defamation?

Generally, a false statement about another intentionally disseminated to others may provide a cause for litigation. There are two types: *libel* and *slander*. **Libel** is the written word defaming another, while **slander** is the publication by any other means.

E. A Law Enforcement Officer's Immunities to Liability

As a law enforcement officer, what protections do I have from exposure to liability?

In addition to some of the issues already discussed above, the following protections should be mentioned:

1. *Good faith*: Good faith involves individuals performing responsibilities with good intentions. *Qualified, good-faith immunity* refers to the fact that a person performing in good faith at the "reasonable person" standard or better generally will be found not liable for his or her actions performed within the scope of his or her duties.

2. *Statutory relief*: An act granting relief or limits on liability may occur in some jurisdictions to protect certain activities of law enforcement officers.

3. *Governmental (or sovereign) immunity*: Common law immunity has been abolished or narrowed in all jurisdictions of the United States. Most states and the United States have tort claims acts allowing individuals to seek relief or restitution from the government.

4. *Information and training*: The most effective defense against liability are proactive measures—adequate information and training. This includes adequate training,

continual maintenance of skills and current information relating to one's duties and responsibilities. As an example, a police officer performing within the reasonable standards of the profession will normally avoid engaging in activities that produce harm.

5. *Insurance*: Liability insurance can be invaluable. It will allow the officer to work in good faith without fear of serious repercussions. Officers should be alert to the exemptions in coverage provided by an insurance policy. It frequently exempts the carrier from paying damages or providing counsel for incidents resulting from criminal behavior, violations of civil rights, and activities outside of the scope of employment or outside of the jurisdiction. Normally, punitive damages are also excluded from coverage.

NOTES

NOTES

members. Procedures for these activities have been worked out and field tested by numerous law enforcement agencies.

Is it legal for law enforcement officers to sell drugs?

This question has been addressed many times and legal opinions and case law indicate that the answer is "yes." Under 21 U.S.C. § 841(a) it is a federal offense to distribute a controlled substance. However, it is generally held that an officer is not criminally liable in this situation because his or her behavior lacks the necessary element of criminal intent. In addition to the legal tradition that would exempt an officer who sells illegal drugs in a reverse sting, federal drug law exists that specifically provides this immunity in 21 U.S.C. § 855(d).

Can reverse sting operations be considered entrapment?

Entrapment occurs when a law enforcement official plants in the mind of an otherwise innocent person the inclination to engage in a criminal act. Merely providing the opportunity to engage in a criminal act, however, does not constitute entrapment.

In the implementation of successful reverse stings, *predisposition* of the potential defendant will remain the critical element should he or she, when prosecuted, claim entrapment. To avoid a court ruling that the officer overstepped his or her duties by inciting or creating the crime, the officer should remain a neutral salesman and allow the buyer's predisposition to control the transaction. It would probably be considered entrapment for the law enforcement officer to encourage or lure a customer with overly zealous selling techniques into buying something the customer doesn't want.

What are some guidelines for reducing the risk of entrapment?

a. When officer-sellers solicit business, they should not mention words such as "crack," "coke," "dope," "grass," "ice," or any other illegal drug.

149

b. Officers should not attempt to encourage a person to buy from them if, at first, he or she denies interest in a drug purchase.

c. Specific people should not be selected for an extra intensive selling effort. The courts have held that targeting specific individuals for sting activities requires a reasonable suspicion that they are likely to engage in the crime. Remember, in the type of "reverse-sting" operation being discussed here, it is not the individual as much as the activity that is being targeted.

What steps are involved in setting up a reverse-sting drug operation?

a. First, it may be necessary to educate those in authority about reverse stings and explain their value in addressing the issue of drug abuse at the particular site. Such an attempt will probably include reassurances concerning the legal aspects of reverse stings, as well as reassurances regarding the public relations implications of such programs.

b. Similarly, the local court and prosecutors with whom the institution works should be brought into the planning discussions.

c. Other area law enforcement agencies should also be contacted and brought into the planning. One valuable strategy (where jurisdictions overlap) is to involve some of these other officers in the reverse stings, thus taking advantage of their experience and sharing with them and their agencies the kudos associated with such undertakings.

d. Where feasible, trustworthy sources in the local media can be contacted and briefed on the plan so that when it is put into operation, there is an increased potential for effective, positive press coverage of what the institution is trying to accomplish.

e.	The selection of the reverse-sting team is a critical component to the program's success. Reverse stings are highly orchestrated operations in which every participant knows exactly what his or her role will be. Each position has a specific name and associated responsibility, and there is a "play-book" by which everyone functions. Members should be volunteers who are physically in shape and adequately trained in self-defense and arrest techniques.

f.	The reverse-sting team must undergo an adequate amount of briefing and scenario training to give the members experience with what they are going to say, how they are going to act as a team, and what they will do should unique types of situations arise. It is wise to videotape this training to provide additional feedback to the participants.

g.	With respect to the drugs that will be sold, decisions have to be made as to their type and sources of supply have to be obtained. Although the particular drugs employed may vary from area to area, most sellers will probably find that it will be necessary to provide cocaine, crack cocaine, and marijuana. With the approval of the court, arrangements can be made through local, state, and federal narcotics enforcement to obtain the drugs. Of course, an accounting system must be established.

h.	In situations in which buyers use motor vehicles to arrive at the selling site, these vehicles may be confiscated. As part of the reverse-sting planning, a procedure (manpower) will be necessary for removing these vehicles from the scene.

i.	Locations for potential reverse stings must be identified and evaluated for their appropriateness. Such factors as exposure to the public, possible escape routes, locations for back-up positioning, and personal safety of the officers, the buyers, and the visiting public must all be taken into account and incorporated into the plan. Also, intelligence must be gathered as to the typical *modus operandi* of drug dealers in the area so these strategies may be duplicated.

GLOSSARY

Accessory After the Fact: An accessory after the fact knows that the felony has been committed and gives aid and comfort to the felons by assisting in their escape, or avoiding detection or arrest.

Accessory Before the Fact: An accessory before the fact is a person who aids, counsels, directs, or orders the commission of a crime but is not present at the time the actual crime is committed. These persons may also be principals in the second degree.

Administrative Arrest: Administrative arrests are based on the same general requirements as conventional arrests and, therefore, they depend on the same foundation. The administrative arrest is different because of its dispositional character rather than its probable cause foundation.

Administrative Frisk: You may frisk a person entering a facility, consistent with institutional or departmental guidelines, because the person may be carrying prohibited items, or materials dangerous to the institution or its personnel.

Adult: A person who has reached his eighteenth birthday, unless declared otherwise by law.

Affidavit: A sworn statement.

Arraignment: The accused is called before the court to hear the formal charges against him and enter a plea.

Arrest: Taking a person into custody or depriving a person of the freedom to come and go because he is a suspect in a particular crime.

Assault: A threat to do bodily harm.

Attempt: An attempt to commit a crime is the action of preparation, but just falling short of completion. An attempted murder may involve injury but does not result in death.

153

Bail: A sum of money set by the judge to insure that the accused will show up and submit to trial.

Battery: The unlawful touching of another, frequently used with assault.

Bench Warrant: A warrant issued from the bench (i.e., a judge in court).

Burden of Proof: The responsibility of the prosecution to prove the accusation with sufficient evidence and, in a criminal case, to establish guilt beyond a reasonable doubt.

Chain of Custody: The protected and documented progression of evidence from the time it is seized until it is admitted at trial. An adequate chain of custody insures the trustworthiness of the evidence.

Change of Venue: The transfer of a court case from one location, such as a county, to another. The motion is made where it appears the venue location is prejudicial or inflamed and the defendant would be denied a fair trail.

Charge: The accusation for which a person is held and tried.

Civil Action: A civil, as opposed to criminal, legal proceeding in which a party seeks some remedy such as money, damages or an injunction.

Color of Law: The figurative cloak or mantle of authority of a public official to carry out the functions of his or her office. It allows a person to act in an official capacity.

Common Law: The law that is derived from the historical customs and court decisions based on those customs as opposed to statutory law.

Competency: The judge will determine the fitness of a witness to testify in a trial or the fitness of documentary or physical evidence to be admitted.

Competent: In criminal matters, the ability to understand the nature and seriousness of the charges and the ability to assist in one's defense.

Complaint: A sworn statement alleging a crime by a particular person.

Conduct: Conduct, in the eyes of the law, includes acts and failure to act.

Consent: A waiver of a constitutional right given with the knowledge of the right not to do so. It must be given freely, intelligently, and without coercion.

Conspiracy: An agreement between two or more people to commit a crime.

Contemporaneous: Occurring at the same time and place.

Contempt of Court: Willful disobedience of a court order.

Continuance: The postponement of a court proceeding to a later date.

Contraband: Property that may not be lawfully possessed and may be lawfully taken by an officer for that reason. This does not normally include real estate.

Corpus Delicti: The object upon which the crime was committed, such as the body of a murder victim or the shell of a boat that was burned.

Credibility: The jury's decision of whether a witness is credible, believable.

Criminal Intent: The criminal intention to knowingly and willfully engage in the criminal act, which is required to establish guilt. Reckless conduct may suffice to demonstrate intent, as may negligent behavior.

Cross-Examination: The in-court questioning of a witness for the opposition to determine the truthfulness and accuracy of the testimony that he or she gave.

Curtilage: The close space around a dwelling that is considered part of the dwelling and is the premises in which there is the highest reasonable expectation of privacy. It is the space that would be found within the "picket fence," and includes close out buildings in which a man or woman could stand, such as a barn, corn crib, chicken house, etc.

Damages: The money compensation awarded the plaintiff in a civil action for an injury or loss. Compensatory damages are for the actual loss or injury, while the punitive damages are over and above that amount to punish the offender and deter repetition of the harmful act.

Delinquent: A juvenile who has committed a crime.

Detention: The temporary holding of a person for the purpose of investigation. The action is for a very short period and does not constitute an arrest.

Double Jeopardy: The United States Constitution prohibition of the prosecution of a person for the same crime by the same jurisdiction more than once unless the matter is appealed by the accused.

Dual Sovereignty: The situation in which a crime offends more than one jurisdiction (sovereign), such as federal and state and either or both could prosecute without violating prohibitions of double jeopardy.

Due Process: The constitutionally guaranteed protections and procedures preventing loss of life, liberty, or property without such proper legal safeguards.

D.U.I.: Driving under the influence, i.e., being under the influence of some intoxicant or drug.

D.W.I.: Driving while intoxicated, which in most jurisdictions is driving while intoxicated by some drug or alcohol.

With alcohol, it is generally a blood level of at least 0.08% or 0.1% by weight depending on the jurisdiction.

Elements of a Crime: Certain elements which must be proven to convict a person of any particular crime. As an example, the elements of burglary (common law or first degree in most states) are the (1) breaking and (2) entering, of the (3) dwelling of (4) another (5) at night, with the (6) intention of committing a felony. All of the elements must be proven plus the fact that the accused did the acts at the time and place stated.

Elephant Rule: The area in which an officer may search, which is confined to the place of need or the place where the item sought is likely to be. If searching for an elephant, you may not look in the glove compartment. If you are searching for narcotics, on the other hand, a glove compartment would probably be an appropriate place to look.

Entrapment: The defense that the accused did the act but that the only reason was that the law enforcement officer tricked or persuaded him to do so. The theory is that the evil intent originated in the mind of the officer who was trying to entrap the accused.

Evidence: The testimony or tangible objects introduced in a trial to convince the jury or judge of the truth of a fact at issue.

Exclusionary Rule: A judicially created rule that allows the defendant or court to suppress (exclude) for trial any evidence, or derivatives thereof, obtained illegally by governmental officers or agents acting under color of law.

Exigent Circumstances: Unusual circumstances allowing quick action where such is not normally permitted. A scream, a shot, the probability that evidence is about to be destroyed immediately and the presence of great immediate danger.

Ex Post Facto: The United States Constitution prohibition of an action being made a crime after it occurs. It also prohibits the increasing of a penalty for the crime after the act.

Extenuating Circumstances: Facts concerning the commission of a crime that may reduce the punishment. This does not excuse the crime; it may only lessen the penalty.

Extradition: The legal process by which one jurisdiction obtains a person for prosecution from another jurisdiction holding the person.

False Arrest: The unlawful detention or holding of a person.

Felony: A serious crime for which the punishment is normally a year or more in prison.

Frisk: A pat down of outer clothing for the purpose of looking for weapons and based on the belief that the suspect may be armed or dangerous. The pat down includes all external clothing and is not a search.

Fruits of a Crime: Items gained from the commission of a crime, e.g., money from the bank robbery.

Fruit of the Poisonous Tree: Otherwise legal and proper evidence obtained as the product of other illegal police activity which is not, as a rule, admissible.

Grand Jury: A group of citizens taken from a cross section of a community by law to hear the presentation of some evidence in a case and determine if there is sufficient probable cause to indict. If the Grand Jury determines that there is sufficient probable cause it hands down an indictment.

Habeas Corpus: A petition by one who believes that he is being held in jail illegally and demanding that the holding authority justify the detention or release him.

Had Reason to Know: An individual, normally a defendant, had such information that a person of at least reasonable intelligence would derive that a particular fact exists.

Harm: When considering liability, a measurable injury to a person, property, or interest.

Hearsay: A statement by one witness of what he heard another person say.

Indictment: The formal written charges against an individual on which the person is brought to trial. The indictment is handed down by the Grand Jury.

Initial Appearance: The first judicial hearing for the accused for the purpose of determining detention, bond or both.

Injury: In discussing liability, an injury is some type of intrusion upon an interest protected by tort law.

Insane: A legal term dealing with the suspect's mental state at the time the offense was committed. A person may be found not guilty by reason of insanity. The theory holds that the insane person's mental state prevented his having the evil intent to commit the act.

Intoxication: Having one's behavior influenced by some chemical such as alcohol. Normally, voluntary intoxication is not a defense to a crime.

Judicial Notice: The judge taking notice of a fact without its having to be proved (e.g., it is dark at midnight).

"Jump and Reach" Rule: The search area immediately around the arrestee where the person in custody might "jump and reach" a weapon or destroy evidence.

Jurisdiction: The authority to inquire into a crime, deal with it through arrest and trial, and pass sentence.

Juvenile: A person who has not reached his eighteenth birthday, unless declared otherwise by law.

Mala in Se: Crimes which are naturally wrong in themselves such as murder, rape, kidnapping, burglary and robbery.

Mala Prohibita: Crimes created by law which are wrong because the acts impose on others or interfere with the orderly operation of society. Examples include: speeding, illegal parking, and walking on the grass.

Malice: The criminal intent or state of mind causing the person to commit the crime.

Mere Suspicion: A hunch, or a feeling based on the officer's experience that something is amiss, which may cause the officer to observe or investigate further. It is not the basis for further action until additional articulable facts elevate the suspicion or knowledge.

Minor: Generally a person who has not reached his eighteenth birthday, unless declared otherwise by law.

Miranda Warning: The Court-mandated warnings that must be given to a suspect prior to in-custody interrogation. These warnings include: (1) the right to remain silent, (2) the right to have an attorney present during interrogation, (3) the right to have a court-appointed attorney if the suspect cannot afford one, and (4) anything the suspect says can be used against him or her in a court of law.

Misdemeanor: A less serious crime for which the punishment is normally less than a year in prison.

Mistrial: A trial which is incomplete because of a deadlocked jury or procedural error. The trial may be held again without double jeopardy interfering.

Modus Operandi, **also M.O.**: The pattern or way of doing something. In criminal matters it normally refers to the pattern of committing the crime by a particular individual or group.

Moving Roadblock: An officer on patrol stopping vehicles or persons in vehicles matching a particular description or a particular need such as permit checks, license checks, etc.

Motive: The reason a person committed the crime.

Negligence: An act or omission of an act that causes harm to another which the reasonably prudent person would not do. This occurs in criminal and civil matters.

Open Fields: The areas outside of a curtilage in which an owner's expectation of privacy is diminished.

Perjury: A statement made under oath in a judicial proceeding, which the person making the statement knows to be false.

Physical harm: In liability, a term which implies abuse of the person or property of another.

Plaintiff: The party bringing suit in a civil action.

Plain View: Items which an officer may observe without moving objects or entering an area in which he or she does not have a right to be. Objects may be observed with the aid of a flashlight, binoculars, etc.

Plea: The accused enters a plea before trial, normally guilty or not guilty or *nolo contendre*. A plea of "guilty" is a total admission to all of the facts of the charge to which it is entered. A "not guilty" plea is a total denial of all facts. The *"nolo contendre"* is a denial for civil purposes but an admission for criminal purposes (I didn't do it and I won't do it again).

Preliminary Hearing: A judicial hearing to determine probable cause to hold an accused and set bail.

Presumption: An inference at law that a fact exists because of another fact.

Presumption of Innocence: A presumption that all persons are innocent even though charged with a crime. This presumption lasts throughout the trial process until the jury returns a verdict of guilty. The state must overcome this presumption by proving beyond a reasonable doubt that the accused committed the particular crime as charged.

Principal: Principals are designated principals in the first or second degree. A principal in the first degree is the person who actually commits the crime. If more than one person commits the crime, all are principals in the first degree. A principal in the second degree is normally absent at the time the crime is committed but aids in the actual commission.

Probable Cause: In arrest, the existence of more reason to believe than not that a particular person committed a particular crime.

Reasonable Suspicion: The belief by an experienced reasonable officer that a crime is about to be, is being, or has been committed (short of probable cause to support an arrest) which gives the officer the grounds to stop, and frisk if appropriate, an individual for a brief investigative time to determine the circumstances and determine if probable cause does in fact exist.

Search Warrant: A court order directing an officer to search a specified location, person or object for particular evidence of a suspected crime and to seize such evidence if it is found.

Self Defense: The defense in a court proceeding that the accused had to use the force in question to defend himself and that he had a right to do so.

Search (of a person): A search conducted pursuant to a warrant and within the scope of the warrant or incident to an arrest. The search incident to arrest is to protect the officer, prevent the destruction of evidence, and prevent escape or suicide.

Search (of an area): The search for particular evidence, contraband, fruits, or instrumentalities of a crime pursuant to (a) a warrant and within the scope and time frame of the warrant, or (b) a search of the immediate surrounding area ("jump and reach" rule) of an arrestee, which is permitted pursuant to the arrest if contemporaneous in time and place.

Should have Known: An aspect of negligence, which holds that a person of reasonable intelligence would know of a particular fact or set of facts and govern his or her behavior accordingly.

Specific Intent: The requirement in some crimes of the proof of specific intent to commit the crime or cause the result, which cannot be presumed from the unlawful act itself.

Statute: Laws enacted by the legislative body and signed into law by the presiding executive, governor, or president.

Statute of Limitations: A statutory creation of a time limit in which an indictment must be filed or the crime may not be prosecuted. Statutes of limitation vary from one jurisdiction to another, but as a rule the more serious crimes are not included and may be prosecuted at any time.

Subpoena: An order of the court commanding the appearance of a person to give testimony and to bring certain objects if so ordered.

Suppression Hearing: A judicial hearing to determine whether or not evidence should be suppressed under the Exclusionary Rule because the evidence is incompetent.

"Terry" Frisk: A frisk that had judicial approval in the case *Terry v. Ohio*; that is, a pat down of outer clothing for the purpose of looking for weapons and based on the belief that the suspect may be armed or dangerous. The pat down includes all external clothing and is not a search. See cases for further information.

Tort: A wrongful act or failure to act which causes injury or loss to another and for which the injured party may sue for damages or injunction.

Unruly Behavior: Behavior peculiar to juveniles that is contrary to law, such as drinking, smoking, being out after curfew, etc.

Venire: The group of citizens from which a jury is drawn.

Venue: The location or site of the crime.

Verdict: A finding by the judge or jury after all of the evidence has been presented.

VIN: Vehicle Identification Number. A number required by law and normally on a plate assigned to a particular vehicle. The number is easily observed and accessible to view and, if covered, may be cleared for viewing by the officer.

RELEVANT LEGAL CASES

ARRESTS

Warrantless Arrests

Payton v. New York, 445 U.S. 573, 100 S.Ct. 1371, 63 L.Ed. 2d 639 (1980): The Fourth Amendment prohibits police from making a warrantless and non-consensual entry into a suspect's home (or premises) in order to make a routine felony arrest. Entry may be made without a warrant only if the officer is in hot pursuit or there are exigent circumstances.

United States v. Watson, 423 U.S. 411, 96 S.Ct. 820, 46 L.Ed.2d 598 (1976): Failure to secure a warrant for an arrest will not invalidate the arrest if it is based on probable cause.

California v. Hodari D., ___ U.S. ___, 111 S.Ct. 1547, 113 L.Ed.2d 690 (1991): If a suspect does not yield to a show of authority, and there is no physical force, there is no seizure of the person. There must be an application of force, however slight, or a show of authority to which a suspect submits, for there to be a seizure of the person.

Hearings

County of Riverside v. McLaughlin, 114 U.S. 49, 111 S.Ct. 1661, 114 L.Ed. 2d 49 (1991): A jurisdiction that has probable cause determination must do so as soon as reasonably feasible, but no more than 48 hours after the arrest.

BAIL:

Stack v. Boyle, 342 U.S. 1, 72 S.Ct. 1, 96 L.Ed. 3 (1951): Bail is excessive if it exceeds the amount necessary to insure the accused's presence at trial.

COUNSEL:

Brewer v. Williams, 430 U.S. 387, 97 S.Ct. 1232, 51 L.Ed.2d 424 (1977): The police may not interrogate once an accused has refused to speak without his attorney being present.

Brown v. Mississippi, 297 U.S. 278, 56 S.Ct. 461, 80 L.Ed. 682 (1936): Confessions obtained by coercion are a violation of due process.

Escobedo v. Illinois, 378 U.S. 478, 84 S.Ct. 1758, 12 L.Ed.2d 977 (1964): Incriminating statements made during an interrogation in which requests for counsel were denied and Miranda warnings were not given are inadmissible at trial.

Gideon v. Wainwright, 372 U.S. 335, 83 S.Ct. 792, 9 L.Ed.2d 799 (1963): An accused is entitled to counsel in a trial.

Massiah v. United States, 377 U.S. 201, 84 S.Ct. 1199, 12 L.Ed.2d 246 (1964): An accused's incriminating words obtained after charges had been filed during an interrogation without benefit of counsel may not be introduced against him in trial.

Spano v. New York, 360 U.S. 315, 79 S.Ct. 1202, 3 L.Ed.2d 1265 (1959): A confession obtained through fatigue and sympathy is involuntary and inadmissible.

DEADLY FORCE:

Tennessee v. Garner, 475 U.S.1, 105 S.Ct. 1694, 85 L.Ed.2d 1 (1985): Deadly force may not be used to effect an arrest. Deadly force may be used only where the officer has reason to believe that the suspect poses a significant threat of death or serious injury to the officer or to others.

ELECTRONIC SURVEILLANCE, INFORMANTS, AND AGENTS:

Hoffa v. United States, 385 U.S. 293, 87 S.Ct. 408, 17 L.Ed.2d 374 (1966): Evidence obtained from a secret informer is valid if the evidence is given voluntarily and based on "misplaced confidence."

Katz v. United States, 389 U.S. 347, 88 S.Ct. 507, 19 L.Ed.2d 576 (1967): A person with a reasonable expectation of privacy is protected by the Fourth Amendment, and a physical trespass without a warrant is a breach of that privacy.

Lewis v. United States, 385 U.S. 206, 87 S.Ct. 424, 17 L.Ed.2d 312 (1966): An agent, under cover, may deceptively enter a premises that has become a commercial center (i.e., selling narcotics) without a warrant and all observations and conversations are legal seizures.

United States v. White, 401 U.S. 745, 91 S.Ct. 1122, 28 L.Ed.2d 453 (1971): The Fourth Amendment does not apply where a person voluntarily confides wrongdoing. A person's expectations of trust are not protected.

ENTRAPMENT:

United States v. Russell, 411 U.S. 423, 93 S.Ct. 1637, 36 L.Ed.2d 366 (1973): The question of entrapment is for the jury, which will assess the defendant's predisposition to commit a crime rather than the type or degree of police conduct.

EXCLUSIONARY RULE:

Mapp v. Ohio: 367 U.S. 643, 81 S.Ct. 1684, 6 L.Ed.2d 1081 (1961): Affirmed the Exclusionary Rule; evidence obtained improperly (in this case, without a valid search warrant) may not be used against a defendant in court.

Segura v. United States, 468 U.S. 796, 104 S.Ct. 3380, 82 L.Ed.2d 599 (1984): The Exclusionary Rule does not apply if the connection between illegal police conduct, discovery, and the resultant seizure of evidence is so "attenuated as to dissipate the taint."

FIRST AMENDMENT:

A Quaker Action Group v. Morton, 516 F.2d 717 (1975): Although some facilities may be reserved for specific purposes, in general, public assembly for First Amendment purposes is a justifiable "park use."

GOOD FAITH:

Malley v. Briggs, 475 U.S. 335, 106 S.Ct. 1092, 89 L.Ed.2d 271 (1986): This case explored the limits of qualified good-faith immunity to alleged Fourth Amendment violations. Even though he had a warrant, the officer was liable for an unconstitutional arrest because he should have known that the facts presented for the warrant did not establish probable cause. Officer must exercise reasonable professional judgment.

SELECTED FIFTH AMENDMENT CASES

Coercion

Arizona v. Fulminante, ___ U.S. ___, 111 S.Ct. 1246, 113 L.Ed.2d 302 (1991): Whether or not a confession is coerced depends on the totality of the circumstances; if, however, a defendant's confession is coerced, its use against the defendant will be reviewed from the beginning (*de novo*) under the harmless error rule.

Informing Suspects of Their Rights

Beckwith v. United States, 425 U.S. 341, 96 S.Ct. 1612, 48 L.Ed.2d 1 (1976): Miranda is not applicable to a non-custodial interrogation that is voluntary in nature.

long as the inventory is done in good faith and not for the purpose of obtaining evidence. Law enforcement officers do not have to offer an arrestee the opportunity to make his or her own arrangements for securing the vehicle; they may impound the vehicle if they wish.

South Dakota v. Opperman, 428 U.S. 364, 96 S.Ct. 3092, 49 L.Ed.2d 100 (1976): A vehicle taken into police custody for protection of the vehicle may be inventoried pursuant to standard police procedures without a warrant.

Florida v. Wells, 495 U.S. 1, 110 S.Ct. 1632, 109 L.Ed.2d 1 (1990): Opening a closed container encountered in a vehicle inventory violates the Fourth Amendment, absent a written policy directing such activity. In no event may the inventory be used as a pretext for uncovering evidence.

JURISDICTION:

Solorio v. U.S., 483 U.S. 435, 107 S.Ct. 2924, 97 L.Ed.2d 364 (1987) The military has jurisdiction over an active duty service member accused of a crime, even if the crime is not service-connected.

JUVENILES

In re Gault, 387 U.S. 1, 87 S.Ct. 1428, 18 L.Ed.2d 527 (1967): While verifying the philosophy for dealing with juveniles, Gault establishes four guarantees for juveniles in the juvenile justice process 1) Notice of charges, 2) Right to Counsel, 3) Right to confrontation and cross-examination, and 4) the Privilege against self-incrimination.

Kent v. United States, 383 U.S. 541, 86 S.Ct. 1045, 16 L.Ed.2d 84 (1966): A juvenile is entitled to a hearing, which may be informal, prior to waiving a juvenile over to be tried as an adult. While the hearing need not conform to all the requirements of a criminal trial or even the usual administrative hearing, it must measure up to the essentials of due process and fair treatment. It includes as a minimum, the right of counsel and the incidents thereto.

New Jersey v. T.L.O., 469 U.S. 325, 105 S.Ct. 733, 83 L.Ed.2d 720 (1985): The Fourth Amendment's prohibition concerning unreasonable searches and seizures applies to searches conducted by school officials. However, accommodation of privacy interests of school children with the substantial need of teachers and administrators for freedom to maintain order in schools does not require strict adherence to the requirement that searches be based on probable cause to believe that the subject of the search has violated or is violating the law. Rather, the legality of the search of a student should depend simply on reasonableness, under all of the circumstances, of the search.

In the Matter of Winship, 397 U.S. 358, 90 S.Ct. 1068, 25 L.Ed.2d 368 (1970): Juveniles, like adults, are constitutionally entitled to proof beyond a reasonable doubt when they are charged with a violation of criminal law.

LINEUPS:

Kirby v. Illinois, 406 U.S. 682, 92 S.Ct. 1877, 32 L.Ed.2d 411 (1972): There is no right to counsel at a lineup before the accused is arrested or charged.

Neil v. Biggers, 409 U.S. 188, 93 S.Ct. 375, 343 L.Ed.2d 401 (1972): A suspect's rights have been violated and the evidence obtained from a lineup may be excluded when the lineup is unduly suggestive.

United States v. Wade, 388 U.S. 218, 87 S.Ct. 1926, 18 L.Ed.2d 1149 (1967): Once an accused has been formally charged he is entitled to counsel at a lineup.

PROBABLE CAUSE:

Draper v. United States, 358 U.S. 307, 79 S.Ct. 329, 3 L.Ed.2d 327 (1959): Probable cause exists when an officer of reasonable caution believes that an offense is being or is about to be committed, based on objective facts and circumstances.

Illinois v. Gates, 462 U.S. 213, 103 S.Ct. 2317, 76 L.Ed.2d 527 (1983): The rigid "two prong test" is abandoned in favor of the "totality of the circumstances test" when determining whether an informant's tip will support probable cause for the issuance of a search warrant. A warrant may be issued on a partially corroborated anonymous informant's tip.

PROTECTIVE SWEEPS:

Maryland v. Buie, 494 U.S. 325, 110 S.Ct. 1093, 108 L.Ed.2d 276 (1990): Police officers need no more than a reasonable suspicion to conduct a protective "sweep" of a dwelling in which they are making a valid arrest.

SEARCHES:

Consent Searches:

Florida v. Jimeno, ___ U.S. ___, 111 S.Ct. 1801, 114 L.Ed.2d 297 (1991): Consent to search a vehicle extends to closed containers found inside of the vehicle that could contain the object of the search. However, it does not normally extend to locked or sealed containers, unless specifically incorporated in the consent.

Schneckloth v. Bustamonte, 412 U.S. 218, 93 S.Ct. 2041, 36 L.Ed.2d 854 (1973): Consent voluntarily given without coercion will permit a lawful search.

Stoner v. California, 376 U.S. 483, 84 S.Ct. 889, 11 L.Ed.2d 856 (1964): Only persons with actual or apparent authority over the premises may consent to a search of the premises.

Illinois v. Rodriguez, 497 U.S. 177, 110 S.Ct. 2793, 111 L.Ed.2d 148 (1990): The police may enter private premises without a warrant if they are acting in reliance upon the consent of a third party whom they reasonably, but mistakenly, believe has common authority over the premises.

Motor Vehicle Searches:

Carroll v. United States, 267 U.S. 132, 45 S.Ct. 280, 69 L.Ed. 543 (1925): A warrantless search of an automobile is permissible where there is probable cause to believe the vehicle may be carrying evidence or the fruits or instrumentalities of a crime.

Chambers v. Maroney, 399 U.S. 42, 90 S.Ct. 1975, 26 L.Ed.2d 419 (1970): Affirmed the right of officers to conduct a warrantless search of an arrested person's motor vehicle after it had been towed to the police station.

New York v. Belton, 453 U.S. 454, 101 S.Ct. 2860, 69 L.Ed. 2d 768 (1981): Incident to the lawful arrest of its occupant, the search of a vehicle's interior passenger compartment may include an examination of the contents of any closed or open containers, including the glove compartment, luggage, boxes, bags, clothing, or any other receptacles.

New York v. Class, 475 U.S. 106, 106 S.Ct. 960, 89 L.Ed.2d 81 (1986): There is no reasonable expectation of privacy in a vehicle identification number (VIN).

United States v. Ross, 456 U.S. 798, 102 S.Ct 2157, 72 L.Ed.2d. 572 (1982): A valid warrantless automobile search may, with probable cause, extend to the containers within the vehicle.

Plain View Doctrine

Horton v. California, 496 U.S. 128 110 S.Ct. 2301, 110 L.Ed.2d 112 (1990): A police officer may make a warrantless seizure of items whose character is "immediately apparent" regardless of whether he had prior reason to believe the items would be encountered. To justify warrantless seizure of an item in plain view, the police officer must not only be lawfully located in a place from which the object can be plainly seen, the officer must also have a lawful right or access to the object itself.

Coolidge v. New Hampshire, 403 U.S. 443, 91 S.Ct. 2022, 29 L.Ed.2d 564 (1971): A valid search warrant is required to search a premises (dwelling) unless there are exigent circumstances. Plain view into a dwelling area is not sufficient for a search.

Arizona v. Hicks, 480 U.S. 321, 107 S.Ct. 1149, 94 L.Ed.2d 347 (1987): Any movement of an object (e.g., turning over a piece of electronics to read its serial number) is a "search" and does not come under the "plain view" exception to the warrant requirement.

Premises Searches

Bumper v. North Carolina, 391 U.S. 543, 88 S.Ct. 1788, 20 L.Ed.2d 797 (1968): A search where police gain consensual admission to a premises through deception by claiming to possess a warrant is unlawful.

California v. Greenwood, 486 U.S.35, 108 S.Ct. 1625 (1988): Placing garbage outside the curtilage (e.g., on the curb or in a campground garbage can) results in a loss of a reasonable expectation of privacy with respect to the contents.

United States v. Dunn, 480 U.S. 294, 107 S.Ct. 1134, 94 L.Ed.2d 326 (1987): The Court found four factors to be considered when determining whether an area is within a curtilage: (1) the proximity of the area to the home, (2) whether the area is included in an enclosure around the home, (3) the nature of uses to which area is put, and (4) the steps taken by resident to protect the area from observation by passersby.

United States v. Matlock, 415 U.S. 164, 94 S.Ct. 988, 39 L.Ed.2d 242 (1974): Any person with an equal right to a premises may consent to a search of the premises.

Roadblocks

Michigan v. Sitz, 496 U.S. 444, 110 S.Ct. 2481, 110 L.Ed.2d 412 (1990): Police may employ highway checkpoint stops as a way of detecting and deterring motorists who drive under the influence of intoxicants. Stopping and briefly detaining all motorists passing through such checkpoints is constitutionally reasonable.

Searches Incident to Arrest

Chimel v. California: 395 U.S. 752, 89 S.Ct. 2034, 23 L.Ed.2d 685 (1969): Limited the scope of a search incident to arrest to the area immediately around the arrestee ("jump and reach" rule).

Hudson v. Palmer, 468 U.S. 517, 104 S.Ct. 3194, 82 L.Ed.2d 393 (1984): An incarcerated prisoner does not have a reasonable expectation of privacy and is, therefore, not protected by the Fourth Amendment's protection against unreasonable searches and seizures. A prisoner's clothes could, therefore, be taken for examination, if the prisoner is provided with replacement clothing.

Illinois v. Lafayette, 462 U.S. 640, 103 U.S. 2605, 77 L.Ed.2d 65 (1983): As a part of a routine procedure for admission to confinement, police may search the individual and his or her personal effects if he or she is under lawful arrest.

United States v. Chadwick, 433 U.S. 1, 97 S.Ct. 2476, 53 L.Ed.2d 538 (1977): Sealed containers seized at the time of arrest may not be searched without a warrant.

United States v. Edwards, 415 U.S. 800, 94 S.Ct. 1234, 39 L.Ed.2d 771 (1974): Pursuant to a lawful arrest, clothing worn by the arrestee may be seized as evidence. The arrestee must be given replacement clothing.

United States v. Robinson, 414 U.S. 218, 94 S.Ct. 467, 38 L.Ed.2d 427 (1973): In the case of a lawful, custodial arrest, a full search of the person and objects within his possession is reasonable and proper without a warrant.

Vale v. Louisiana, 399 U.S. 30, 90 S.Ct. 1969, 26 L.Ed.2d 409 (1970): A warrantless search made incident to arrest must be confined to the immediate vicinity of the arrest (jump and reach rule).

Warrant Searches

Davis v. Mississippi, 394 U.S. 721, 89 S.Ct. 1394, 22 L.Ed.2d 676 (1969): Illegally seized evidence is inadmissible at trial.

Hayes v. Florida, 470 U.S. 811, 105 S.Ct. 1643, 84 L.Ed.2d 705 (1985): An individual's Fourth Amendment rights are violated when he is forcibly removed from a place he is entitled to be in order to obtain fingerprints, and the officers are acting without probable cause and judicial supervision.

Massachusetts v. Sheppard, 468 U.S. 981, 104 S.Ct. 3424, 82 L.Ed. 2d 737 (1984): When police officers take every reasonable step to obtain a valid search warrant from a detached, neutral magistrate who assures the officers of the warrant's validity, and when the officers proceed to enforce the warrant, acting in good faith, the evidence will be admissible even though the warrant is subsequently determined to be invalid.

United States v. Leon, 468 U.S. 897, 104 S.Ct. 3405, 82 L.Ed.2d 677 (1984): The Exclusionary Rule does not bar the use of evidence obtained by officers acting in good-faith reasonable reliance on a search warrant issued by a detached and neutral magistrate but ultimately found to be invalid.

Warden v. Hayden, 387 U.S. 294, 87 S.Ct. 1642, 18 L.Ed.2d 782 (1967): A search warrant is the means to search for specific items and does not provide access to a premises to shop for evidence to convict. The duration of the search is for the minimum time to discover the sought items.

Wong Sun v. United States, 371 U.S. 471, 83 S.Ct. 407, 9 L.Ed.2d 441 (1963): Evidence obtained through a lawful search, but based on illegally obtained information or evidence may be excluded as "fruit of the poisonous tree." If the connection between illegal police conduct and the challenged evidence is so removed in time and place or person so as to dissipate the taint, the evidence is admissible.

Warrantless Searches

Andresen v. Maryland, 427 U.S. 463, 96 S.Ct. 2737, 49 L.Ed.2d 627 (1976): The Fifth Amendment protection against self incrimination attaches to the person not to information that may incriminate him.

Cupp v. Murphy, 412 U.S. 291, 93 S.Ct. 2000, 36 L.Ed.2d 900 (1973): Fingernail scrapings taken without consent and absent a formal arrest are constitutional.

Dunaway v. New York, 442 U.S. 200, 99 S.Ct. 2248, 60 L.Ed.2d 824 (1979): The Fourth Amendment is violated when a person is taken into custody, detained and questioned without probable cause. Evidence obtained from such a custodial questioning is inadmissible.

Minnesota v. Olson, 495 U.S. 91, 110 S.Ct. 1684, 109 L.Ed. 2d 85 (1990): A guest in a home has a legitimate expectation of privacy in the residence and is, therefore, entitled to the protection of the Fourth Amendment against police intrusion on that interest.

Schmerber v. California, 384 U.S. 757, 86 S.Ct. 1826, 16 L.Ed.2d 908 (1966): Where evidence in the blood could be destroyed by delay, a warrant is not necessary to take a blood sample. The Fifth Amendment prohibition on self incrimination applies only to items of a testimonial nature.

United States v. Dionisio, 410 U.S. 1, 93 S.Ct. 764, 35 L.Ed. 2d 67 (1973): Non-testimonial evidence is not protected by the Fourth Amendment's prohibition against unreasonable searches and seizures. Examples of non-testimonial evidence include such things as: fingerprinting, photographing, measurements, requests to write or speak for identification, stand, assume a stance, to engage in a particular task, make a particular gesture, or appear in a lineup.

STOP AND FRISK

Adams v. Williams, 407 U.S. 143, 92 S.Ct. 1921, 32 L.Ed.2d 612 (1972): An informant's tip may be sufficient for a stop and frisk even though it would be inadequate to support an arrest warrant. The officer must have a reasonable belief that criminal activity is afoot and the informant's tip must bear some indication of reliability.

Alabama v. White, 496 U.S. 325, 110 S. Ct. 2412, 110 L. Ed. 2d 301 (1990): The combination of an anonymous tip, which alleged that the defendant was about to transport cocaine in a car, and a police officer's corroboration of some of the tip's details provided reasonable suspicion for stopping the vehicle.

Brown v. Texas: 443 U.S. 47, 99 S.Ct. 2637, 61 L.Ed.2d 357 (1979): A person may not be forcibly stopped for mere suspicion. He may be stopped for reasonable (articulable) suspicion.

Terry v. Ohio: 392 U.S. 1, 88 S.Ct. 1868, 20 L.Ed.2d 889 (1968): Established the right of law enforcement officers to stop and frisk individuals whom they reasonably suspect of being involved in criminal activity and that they believe may be armed and dangerous.

United States v. Sharpe, 470 U.S. 675 105 S.Ct. 1568, 84 L.Ed.2d 605 (1985): A suspect may be detained for a brief period while officers conduct an investigation, provided the officers' actions are justified and limited to the needs under the circumstances.

SURVEILLANCE

California v. Ciraolo, 476 U.S. 207, 106 S.Ct. 1809, 90 L.Ed.2d 210 (1986): There is no reasonable expectation of privacy from aerial surveillance, even within a curtilage.

Oliver v. United States, 466 U.S. 170, 104 S.Ct. 1735, 80 L.Ed.2d 214 (1984): Open fields do not provide the setting for those intimate activities that the Fourth Amendment is intended to protect from governmental interference or surveillance. The Fourth Amendment does not protect merely subjective expectations of privacy, but only those expectations that society is prepared to recognize as reasonable.

THE CONSTITUTION OF THE UNITED STATES

SELECTED AMENDMENTS

from

THE BILL OF RIGHTS
(AMENDMENTS 1, 4, 5, 6, 8)

and the

FOURTEENTH AMENDMENT
SECTIONS 1 AND 5

AMENDMENT I

Congress shall make no law respecting an establishment of religion, or prohibiting the free exercise thereof; or abridging the freedom of speech, or of the press; or the right of the people peaceably to assemble, and to petition the Government for a redress of grievances.

. . . . .

AMENDMENT IV

The right of the people to be secure in their persons, houses, papers, and effects, against unreasonable searches and seizures, shall not be violated, and no Warrants shall issue, but upon probable cause, supported by Oath or affirmation, and particularly describing the place to be searched, and the persons or things to be seized.

AMENDMENT V

No person shall be held to answer for a capital, or otherwise infamous crime, unless on a presentment or indictment of a Grand Jury, except in cases arising in the land or naval forces, or in the Militia, when in actual service in time of War or public danger; nor shall any person be subject for the same offence to be twice put in jeopardy of life or limb; nor shall be compelled in any criminal case to be a witness against himself, nor be deprived of life, liberty, or property, without due process of law; nor shall private property be taken for public use, without just compensation.

AMENDMENT VI

In all criminal prosecutions, the accused shall enjoy the right to a speedy and public trial, by an impartial jury of the State and district wherein the crime shall have been committed, which district shall have been previously ascertained by law, and to be informed of the nature and cause of the accusation; to be confronted with the witnesses against him; to have compulsory process for obtaining witnesses in his favor, and to have the Assistance of Counsel for his defence.

. . . . .

AMENDMENT VIII

Excessive bail shall not be required, nor excessive fines imposed, nor cruel and unusual punishments inflicted.

. . . . .

AMENDMENT XIV

Section 1. All persons born or naturalized in the United States, and subject to the jurisdiction thereof, are citizens of the United States and of the State wherein they reside. No State shall make or enforce any law which shall abridge the privileges or immunities of the citizens of the United States; nor shall any State deprive any person of life, liberty, or property, without due process of law; nor deny to any person within its jurisdiction the equal protection of the laws.

. . . . .

Section 5. The Congress shall have power to enforce, by appropriate legislation, the provisions of this article.

. . . . .

SELECTED PERTINENT STATUTES

from the

UNITED STATES CODE

18 U.S.C. §242 Deprivation of rights under color of law

Whoever, under color of any law, statute, ordinance, regulation, or custom, willfully subjects any inhabitant of any State, Territory or District to the deprivation of any rights, privileges, or immunities secured or protected by the Constitution or laws of the United States, or to different punishments, pains, or penalties, on account of such inhabitant being an alien, or by reason of his color, or race, than are prescribed for the punishment of citizens, shall be fined not more than $1,000 or imprisoned not more than one year, or both; and if death results shall be subject to imprisonment for any term of years or for life.

42 U.S.C. §1983 Civil action for deprivation of rights

Every person who, under color of any statute, ordinance, regulation, custom, or usage, of any State or Territory, subjects, or causes to be subjected, any citizen of the United States or other person within the jurisdiction thereof to the deprivation of any rights, privileges, or immunities secured by the Constitution and laws, shall be liable to the party injured in an action at law, suit in equity, or other proper proceeding for redress.